TACOMA RAIL

ONE HUNDRED YEARS AND STILL ON TRACK

TACOMA

RAIL

100
YEARS

1914

2014

The 2200s poised on the ready track. These units were purchased using a 2011 Environmental Protection Agency grant to replace the older, less efficient GP20s.

THE
DONNING COMPANY
PUBLISHERS

TACOMA RAIL

ONE HUNDRED YEARS AND STILL ON TRACK

STUART WADE

The Donning Company Publishers
184 Business Park Drive, Suite 206
Virginia Beach, VA 23462

Lex Cavanah, General Manager
Nathan Stufflebean, Production Supervisor
Anne Burns, Editor
Jeremy Glanville, Graphic Designer
Monika Ebertz, Imaging Artist
Kathy Snowden Railey, Project Research Coordinator
Katie Gardner, Marketing Advisor

James H. Railey, Project Director

Library of Congress Cataloging-in-Publication Data

Names: Wade, Stuart.
Title: Tacoma Rail : one hundred years and still on track / by Stuart Wade.
Description: Virginia Beach, VA : The Donning Company Publishers, 2016. |
    Includes bibliographical references and index.
Identifiers: LCCN 2015050576 | ISBN 9781681840192
Subjects: LCSH: Tacoma Rail--History. | Street-railroads--Washington
    (State)--Tacoma--History. | Railroads--Washington (State)--Tacoma
    Region--History. | Tacoma (Wash.)--History--20th century. | Tacoma
    (Wash.)--History--21st century. | Tacoma Region (Wash.)--History.
Classification: LCC TF725.T33 W33 2016 | DDC 388.4/6065797788--dc23
LC record available at http://lccn.loc.gov/2015050576

Printed in the United States of America at Walsworth

TABLE OF **CONTENTS**

FOREWORD

William A. Gaines, Director/CEO of Tacoma Public Utilities. *Photo by Rick Dahms*

As we move into Tacoma Rail's second century of operation we thought it would be appropriate to look back on its first hundred years of providing service that is vital to the economic health of the community.

The smallest of the three divisions that comprise Tacoma Public Utilities, Tacoma Rail prides itself on being different. A publicly owned short line in an industry dominated by privately held, for-profit rail carriers, Tacoma Rail's cost-of-service business model has enabled it to survive and indeed thrive in an era that has seen innumerable railroads disappear from the scene.

Serving the Port of Tacoma, which bills itself as the "economic engine" of Pierce County, Tacoma Rail views itself as the transmission and drive train that makes the entire system go. With only 30 miles of its own track in a 100-mile terminal complex, Tacoma Rail keeps freight moving efficiently through the port with a solid history of accuracy and timeliness.

Tacoma Rail has positioned itself well for the future. A solid business plan, good relationships with our Class 1 railroad partners, and a willingness to be nimble when needed will keep the railroad tuned up and ready for the inevitable ups and downs of the economy.

In the railroad business, one of the chief assets is employees. Although a small railroad, Tacoma Rail employs some of the best. I have every confidence Tacoma Rail's stellar management team and talented workforce will work hard to make the next 100 years even better than the first.

A 2003 aerial view of the Port of Tacoma prior to the completion of the Pierce County Terminal.
Courtesy of Port of Tacoma

ACKNOWLEDGMENTS

This book is built on a year of research during which I delved into numerous archives, interviewed current and former employees and friends of the organization, and sifted through innumerable book, newspaper, and magazine clippings.

The project springs from kindnesses extended by many people, from friends and family to librarians, fellow writers, and historians. Dale King and his entire Tacoma Rail staff rolled out the red carpet. At Donning, Anne Burns edited this book and was sure-handed. Jeanie Fisher of Tacoma Public Library saved me from professional embarrassment. Special thanks go to rail scribes David Cantlin and Paul Curtiss and photographer Steve Carter for their expertise.

Like many historians, I made existing information written by others central to my research. Probably the best single source was John S. Ott's 1994 *The Story of the Tacoma Municipal Belt Line Railway*, the TMBL-commissioned predecessor to this book. I owe Mr. Ott a major debt of gratitude.

While some sections of this book relied on previous works, others derive from personal interviews I was fortunate to conduct. Thank you Josh Banks, Max Chabo, Roz Crawford, Lori Daniels, Tim Flood, Bill Gaines, Alan Hardy, Clayton Hoffman, Kyle Kellem, Alan Matheson, Dan McCabe, Shawn Merrill, Ron Mills, Marc Robertson, John Roberts, and John Say. Thank you, Dennis Dean and Jonas Simonis, for your time and thoughtful remembrances. My thanks also to Lena Bentley and Jim Railey. Special thanks to Bronmin Shumway, who made the key introductions.

Without mentor extraordinaire Liz Carmack, this book would not exist. Thank you, Liz!

Last but not least, Christi, Ben, John, and Rob Wade are the best family a guy could want. My siblings Woody Wade and Seattle resident Cynthia Lungmus (and husband Perry) each played a big role, as they always do. Many thanks to my parents, Sue and the late James Wade, and to John and the late Jeanie Clark, who provided much more than I could ever repay.

Stuart Wade
Austin, Texas
December 1, 2015

TACOMA RAIL

Ring Bell for Exceptional Service

An aerial view of the Port of Tacoma, with Pierce County Terminal (green cranes) at top center, and Tacoma Rail located at bottom right. Tacoma Rail's core has always been the Tidelands Division, where 95 percent of its business originates and/or terminates within the Tacoma Rail network's first five miles.

CHAPTER ONE

Tacoma Rail is a survivor. What began in 1914 as a modest trolley service is now a key driver of Tacoma's regional economy, fueling more than a century's worth of continuous economic growth at the southern base of Puget Sound.

One hundred years after the municipally owned railroad was created, its distinctive, red and white, 4,300-horsepower locomotives still rumble along the same routes once traced by its horse-drawn streetcars. According to the American Short Line and Regional Railroad Association, Tacoma Rail is now a Class III short line railroad—a publicly owned and self-supported division of Tacoma Public Utilities with annual operating revenue of $28 million.

Tacoma Rail's core has always been the Tidelands Division of Tacoma, where 95 percent of its business originates and/or terminates within the network's first five miles. More recently, however, the railroad added two divisions. This expanded Tacoma Rail from a local terminal road to a regional carrier, serving Pierce, Thurston, and Lewis Counties. The railroad's three divisions—the Capital, the Mountain, and the Tidelands—serve a variety of customers on 204 miles of track.

Signing Belt Line Contracts

The signing of the belt line contract on October 29, 1924. Flanked by railroad executives, Ernest Dolge, the chairman of the Tacoma Chamber of Commerce Traffic and Transportation Committee, is pictured signing the papers. Tacoma Mayor A. V. Fawcett is seated at far left. *Courtesy Tacoma Public Library*

The view of Tacoma in 1884, a short time before the official arrival of the Northern Pacific. Within five years, bustling waterfront, rail, and related Tideflats industrial development (to the east, or right in map), along with the arrival of other major railroads, would drive the population of this formerly sleepy town to 30,000. *Library of Congress, Geography and Map Division*

Tacoma Rail performs the terminal switching operations on behalf of major Class I carriers BNSF Railway and Union Pacific Railroad as well as about 50 customers in its Tidelands Division and works with another 20 customers between the two, newer inland divisions. Industries served include energy, international intermodal containers, automobiles, chemicals, lumber, and aerospace.

The railroad moves much of the freight coming into and out of the Port of Tacoma. From dockside tracks, Tacoma Rail brings railcars to a large classification yard, where crews assemble them into trains bound for like destinations. Eastbound freight goes to rail customers across the United States, carried by the major Class I freight railroads.

Tacoma Rail serves major Class I carriers BNSF Railway and Union Pacific as well as about 50 customers in its Tidelands Division and works with another 20 customers between the two, newer inland divisions.

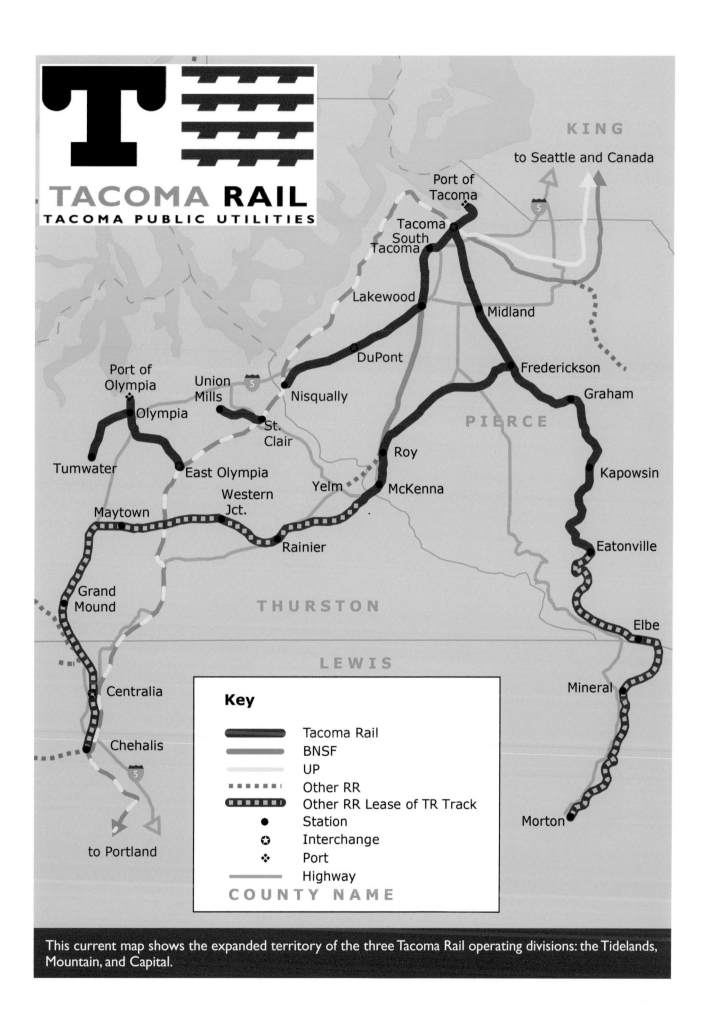

TACOMA RAIL
TACOMA PUBLIC UTILITIES

KING

to Seattle and Canada

Port of Tacoma

Tacoma
South Tacoma

Lakewood

Midland

DuPont

Frederickson

Port of Olympia

Union Mills

Nisqually

Graham

Olympia

St. Clair

PIERCE

Tumwater

East Olympia

Yelm

Roy

Kapowsin

Western Jct.

McKenna

Maytown

Rainier

Eatonville

Grand Mound

THURSTON

Elbe

LEWIS

Centralia

Mineral

Chehalis

Key

▬▬▬	Tacoma Rail
▬▬▬	BNSF
▬▬▬	UP
▪▪▪▪	Other RR
▰▰▰	Other RR Lease of TR Track
●	Station
✪	Interchange
❖	Port
▬▬	Highway

COUNTY NAME

to Portland

Morton

This current map shows the expanded territory of the three Tacoma Rail operating divisions: the Tidelands, Mountain, and Capital.

On the Capital Division line, passing by the state capital building in Olympia.

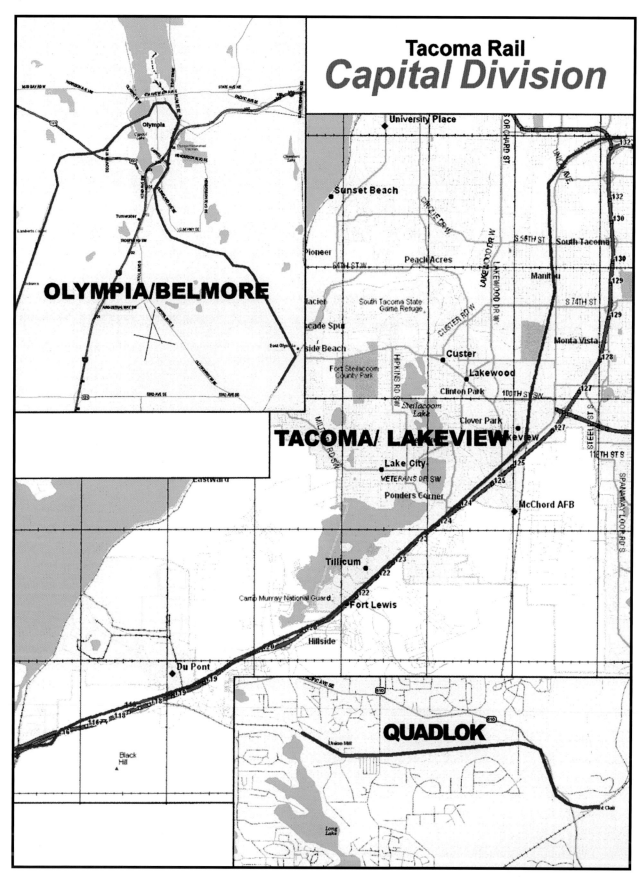

Tacoma Rail
Capital Division

OLYMPIA/BELMORE

TACOMA/ LAKEVIEW

QUADLOK

A map of the Capital Division. Consisting of three disconnected branch lines, the Belmore (running from East Olympia to Belmore), the Quadlok (St. Clair to Quadlok), and Lakeview (Nisqually Junction to South Tacoma), the division was established in 2004 through the lease of two BNSF Railway branch lines and the purchase of the freight franchise on another.

The 1977 staff poses with the Tacoma Municipal Belt Line 950 before the new red/white paint scheme is implemented. Dennis Dean is at the bottom right.

Tacoma Municipal Belt Line employees gather on the SW9 switch engine 1201 in 1990. Twenty-five years later when the centennial was celebrated all these fine railroaders pictured had moved on to other post-Tacoma Rail pursuits.

A "family portrait" taken in November 2014, with about one-third of Tacoma Rail's employees gathered around SD70 ACe 7001.

This resilient little railroad can't be underestimated. Although it remains at the mercy of economic and political forces outside its control, over the decades it has overcome indebtedness, insolvency, poor infrastructure, labor unrest, and threats to absorb it into either other governmental entities or major rail carriers. Weathering recession, aided by the rise of intermodal shipping (the movement of container cargo from one mode of transportation to another), and bolstered by the addition of the two newer rail divisions helping its bottom line, Tacoma Rail has blossomed from an approximate $8 million annual operation just 20 years ago into a $28 million enterprise today.

With 115 employees in 2015, Tacoma Rail is a taxpayer, as opposed to being taxpayer-supported. Rarely, if ever, is profit built into Tacoma Rail's rates. Tacoma Rail is a cost-of-service business, offering customers the freight services that enable them to create jobs and support the tax base for the City of Tacoma.

What set the stage for Tacoma Rail's latter-day success was a 1980's union between the short line railroad the Port of Tacoma operated and the City's Belt Line (a short line railroad operation within and around a city and connecting with one or more larger railroads). When the Port dropped rail service, allowing Tacoma Rail to operate in the Port, the result was a successful partnership and three decades of strong growth for both entities.

Business boomed as industries grew, and Tacoma became the sixth-largest container port in North America. Tacoma remains the state's third-most populous city behind Seattle and Spokane. Today Tacoma Rail's revenue is at an all-time high, fueled by increases in shipping activity and new business in the form of oil shipments from North Dakota to U.S. Oil & Refining in the Tacoma Tideflats. In 2015, the line switched 250,000 railcars and paid $4 million in taxes and assessments to the City.

The SD70 ACe's 7001 and 7002 head east with commercial business for customers in Frederickson, Washington, in 2014. *Photo by Steve Carter*

Acquired in November 2014, the TMBL 7001 is one of the two newest members of the locomotive roster. *Photo by Steve Carter*

Tacoma Rail's "old hill power," SD40's 3000 and 3001, begin the long pull through the compound curves of the gulch with rail sanders full-open to maximize traction. *Photo by David Cantlin*

The "new hill power" heads back down the gulch for the second half of a 3,500-ton train securely tied down in the coach yard. *Photo by Steve Carter*

TIMELINE

1873	Northern Pacific selects Tacoma
1887	Tacoma Street Railway Company—Stampede Pass tunnel
1890	Tacoma Railway & Motor Company—Electricity
1898	Tacoma Railway & Power Company (New Jersey)
	Tideflats "street railway for the workingman"
1914	Birth of municipal rail in Tacoma
1917	War jobs and night freight
1918	Voters establish Port of Tacoma
1919	Tacoma Municipal Street Railway
1925	Name changes to Tacoma Municipal Belt Line (TMBL)
1938	Streetcars out, buses in
1943	Passenger service peaks at 150,000 per month
1944	First diesel-electric locomotives
1945	Rise of freight: new classification yard
1947	City gives passenger service to Tacoma Transit Company (Pierce Transit)
1948–1957	Deferred maintenance, tiny rate increases
1953	City erases 35-year TMBL debt
1958	Possible sale to Port of Tacoma results in rate increase
1960	Carriers offer purchase, but price too low
1962	City budget crunch, sale offer to Port of Tacoma
	Due diligence not followed, no sale
1964	Another Port of Tacoma offer
	City council rejected, offer too small
1969	New classification yard and headquarters
1984	Tariff based on cost of service
1985	Two-year port-rail trial merger under TMBL
1990	TMBL and Port of Tacoma rail merger formalized
1995	Log traffic ends
1998	TMBL name changes to Tacoma Rail
1999	Hyundai infrastructure and rate restructure
2000	Mountain Division established
2004	Capital Division established
2005	Pierce County Terminal (PCT) open for business
	Tacoma Rail switching achieves all-time high
2008	The Great Recession
2011	Mountain Division agreement to transfer of ownership
	First new locomotive ever acquired by Tacoma Rail
2012	Grand Alliance and U.S. Oil help account for first $2 million revenue month
2013	Twenty-year operating agreement is established
	between the Port of Tacoma and Tacoma Rail
2014	Tacoma Rail centennial and the start of another 100 years of success

Northern Pacific Headquarters at 621 Pacific Avenue, circa 1889. The railroad had chosen Tacoma as its western terminus in 1873; from that point, the quiet town would expand to 30,000 citizens by 1890. Northern Pacific sold the building, which stands today and is now an office, to the City of Tacoma in 1922. *Photograph courtesy of the John Ogden Collection. Courtesy Tacoma Public Library, JOGDEN10*

STEEL WHEELS IN TACOMA

CHAPTER TWO

To understand Tacoma Rail in this centennial year of municipal rail in Tacoma, one must first get a sense of the people and the place responsible for producing this railroad, which has been reliably moving passengers and freight across the Tideflats of South Puget Sound for a century.

In 1873, Ulysses Grant entered his second term as president and San Francisco businessman Levi Strauss patented copper-riveted blue jeans. In Adair, Iowa, 25-year-old Jesse James committed his first robbery—a train job, no less—by stealing $3,000 from the Rock Island Express. Central Park was completed. A few months later and a few city blocks away at New York's Hippodrome, P. T. Barnum's "Greatest Show on Earth" made its debut.

BOOMTOWN

That same year, Charles Wright, owner of the Northern Pacific Railway, chose Tacoma (over Seattle or Olympia) as his railway's western terminus. It was no secret the Northern Pacific had been looking for a western capital. However, exactly where on Puget Sound (which still offers the Pacific Coast's only safe and accessible U.S. harbors north of San Francisco) the line would terminate was decided based on the post-Civil War economy as well as geography.

Two other, equally important factors in Northern Pacific's selection of Tacoma were its good harbor, without rocks, shoals, or breakers, and the availability of cheap land the Northern Pacific could acquire for shore facilities. The final two candidates were Seattle and Tacoma. Why did Tacoma come out on top? Where Seattle could offer about 2,500 acres within the city, only 4,800 feet of it fronted on navigable water. Tacoma, on the other hand, had earmarked 2,700 acres with an unbroken two-mile waterfront.

This 1878 entry in *Hunt's History of Tacoma* includes the following: "One can scarcely comprehend the excitement . . . when [Northern Pacific Railroad] President Charles B. Wright sent a telegram to [N.P.] Superintendent Samuel A. Black, saying that the railroad directors had determined to push the line across the Cascades."

In spurning the other potential terminus sites, Wright saw what professional developer Morton Matthew McCarver, founder of Tacoma, had recognized in the 1860s: a deep-water port, access to Snoqualmie Pass, and abundant natural resources nearby would be an ideal place for a railroad.

The City of Tacoma was incorporated following the merger of Old Tacoma and New Tacoma on January 7, 1884. In the 1870s, the impending arrival of a major railway in Tacoma was a monumental event, one far more stupendous, for those times, than anything that could be imagined as a modern-day equivalent—other than, perhaps, the opening of a giant new international airport or the advent of a futuristic "Spaceport on the Sound."

For a one-sawmill, one-school, wilderness of woods—so small it had been mocked in the newspapers for its lack of paint and over-surplus of mud and stumps—this was big news and everyone knew it. Public finances "were not in good order," with the City $4,000 in debt and a dwindling school fund. And it had no overland access to the outside world. To reach the relative "backwater" of Tacoma from points east, one had to travel first to Portland.

All of this soon changed. The completion of the main Northern Pacific line across the Cascade Mountains enabled direct connection, for the first time ever, to anyone traveling to Puget Sound, British Columbia,

Tacoma in 1910, looking south from a location on the steep slope between South Cliff Avenue and Pacific Avenue. The image shows the railroad yard ("Half Moon yard"), the Tacoma Tideflats, and Mount Rainier. Old Tacoma City Hall stands at far right with the Northern Pacific Headquarters across the street.
Courtesy Tacoma Public Library, RICHARDS 5

Alaska, or even Asia. Speculation brought with it people, money, new construction, and demand. Within a decade, Tacoma's population skyrocketed from 1,098 in 1880 to more than 36,000 in 1890, making it one of America's fastest-growing cities.

Rudyard Kipling visited in 1889, stating Tacoma was "literally staggering under a boom of the boomiest." In *Coast to Coast*, his book on American travel, the then 24-year-old Englishman reported:

> I do not quite remember what her natural resources were . . . they included coal and iron, carrots, potatoes, lumber, shipping and a crop of thin newspapers all telling Portland that her days were numbered.

> The crude boarded pavements of the main streets rumbled under the heels of hundreds of furious men all actively engaged in hunting drinks and eligible corner-lots. They sought the drinks first.

> Overhead the drunken telegraph, telephone and electric-light wires tangled on tottering posts . . . Down the muddy, grimy, unmetalied thoroughfare ran a horse-car line; the metals three inches above road level. Beyond this street rose many hills, and the town was thrown like a broken set of dominoes over all.

> The hotel stationery advertised that Tacoma bore on its face all the advantages of the highest civilization, and the newspapers sang the same tune in a louder key.

Masted vessels in this 1901 photograph are waiting on the City Waterway to take on cargo. The buildings on the crowded waterfront are wheat warehouses. The Northern Pacific Headquarters building is at far left upper edge. *Courtesy Tacoma Public Library, G50.1-104*

A view of Buffelen Lumber & Manufacturing Company in November 1921, looking toward Tacoma across the Tideflats. The narrow bridge built on pilings is the old Hylebos Creek bridge. *Courtesy Tacoma Public Library, B4952*

Down in the Tideflats, wheat, coal, and the lumber industry in particular began booming. In addition, some 20-odd mills in the area were processing the surrounding old-growth forest, which was harvested for local use or sent overseas. Before long, the city also attracted several other transcontinental railroads to serve the fast-growing commerce at both its waterfront docks and its industrial Tideflats.

A quick game of "parallel universe" helps illustrate the significance of Northern Pacific's decision to go with Tacoma. The small community of Union in Mason County, Washington, lies along the southern shore of Hood Canal, in an area known as "the Great Bend." The town is so named because the Union Pacific was at one time supposedly going to make its western terminus there. The deal never went through, and the Union Pacific never arrived. The tiny hamlet never developed, and in 2010, the U.S. Census reported a population of 631.

THE BIG BOYS

Northern Pacific was merely the first major carrier to arrive on the scene. The Union Pacific (1910), the Chicago, Milwaukee, St. Paul (also known as the "Milwaukee Road") (1909), and Great Northern (1910) followed soon after. All built transcontinental connections to Tacoma's Commencement Bay, an "excellent little bay," which, at five miles in length and three miles in width, is landlocked and well protected.

The Union Pacific leased the entire Oregon Railroad and Navigation Company line in 1886. By 1890, the Union Pacific owned half of the line and by 1889 was pulling in to Spokane. There was a failed attempt in 1890 to extend a line from Portland into Tacoma before the panic of 1893. Eventually it reached Tacoma through trackage rights on a Northern Pacific line.

Present-day Union, Washington, helps illustrate the significance of Northern Pacific's 1873 decision to go with Tacoma as its western terminus. The scenic area in Mason County, Washington, lies along the southern shore of Hood Canal, in an area known as "the Great Bend." The town is so named because the Union Pacific was at one time supposedly going to choose it over Tacoma and others. The deal never went through, and the UP never arrived. The tiny hamlet never developed, and in the 2010 U.S. Census it reported a population of 631. *Photo by Jody Gripp*

The crew of a Tacoma Eastern steam locomotive pose outside Mineral, Washington, in 1908. In 1919, the Milwaukee Road took control of the Tacoma Eastern line for the next 60 years. Weyerhaeuser bought it in 1980, operating it as the Chehalis Western, moving logs to the port until 1992. Three years later, the City of Tacoma bought and renamed the line the Mountain Division, after the 3.3 percent grade up the Tacoma Gulch. *Courtesy Tacoma Public Library, BROWNING 092*

The now renamed "Chicago, Milwaukee, St. Paul & Pacific Railroad" stretched for 2,200 miles—from Chicago to the ports of Seattle and Tacoma, where it kept a substantial terminal and car shops. The Milwaukee Road also had gained access to some of the best timberland in western Washington through control of the old Tacoma Eastern Railroad—a route later to become Weyerhaeuser property and still later to become the Tacoma Rail "Mountain Division." Formerly the longest railroad in the United States, Milwaukee Road filed for bankruptcy in 1977 and abandoned its Pacific lines in 1980.

Northern Pacific's connecting of Tacoma's adjacent deep-water Commencement Bay and its port with the railroad gave the city its motto, "Where Rails meet Sails," as well as the nickname, "City of Destiny." Today, Commencement Bay still hosts the bustling Port of Tacoma, a center of international trade on the Pacific coast and the largest port in Washington state.

It was the transcontinental rail that enabled the population of the country's Northwest to grow by leaps and bounds in the early years of the twentieth century, as people left the Midwest and points east to make a new life in Montana, Idaho, and Washington. Along with those first NP trains rolling into Tacoma came countless workers and opportunity-seekers, eager to put down roots. All these people had places to be, and so Tacoma also saw the arrival of numerous streetcar companies speculating on the profitability of connecting downtown to Tacoma's new and growing neighborhoods.

From newest to oldest—TMBL 7002 to TMBL 2006 (designated for a rebuild), 2014. *Photo by Steve Carter*

A nice family portrait, 2015.
Photo by Steve Carter

The 7002 does a little night work in the yard, 2015. *Photo by Steve Carter*

The newly arrived TMBL 2100 and the recently refurbished Polson Logging Company #70 Baldwin Mikado steam locomotive owned by Mount Rainier Scenic Railroad rest on the west end of the classification yard after handling the 2011 Tacoma Open House excursion train.

STREET RAIL AND TIDEFLATS

CHAPTER THREE

Over the next two decades—1880 to 1900—more than 20 street transit purveyors rolled the dice in hopes of dominating the Tacoma street rail business, and an astonishing 300 different entities devoted to rail called Tacoma home.

Despite this enormous number of competitors—or because of it—only a handful of these companies ever actually laid a tie or put wheels on rails. Most going concerns either went belly up or—if lucky—were acquired by larger players. The biggest attraction was the Tideflats, its labor force, and its connection with the major railroad lines and shipping lines.

FOUNDING FATHERS

Home Lumber Company held the distinction of being the first local company to locate operations in the Tideflats, setting up operations in 1885. Taken over by J. F. Hart and Company a year later, the organization believed in the location as a great place to have a business.

Also in 1885, the Tacoma and Columbia River Railway and Power Company (the earliest predecessor of the Tacoma Railway and Power Company) built a line from downtown to Edison, where the Northern Pacific had set up its shops, out to Spanaway Park for the development of Spanaway land. The development's promoters touted the area, which was home to few businesses for its "rural living" and "easy access" back to Tacoma and its jobs.

Allen Charles Mason, a successful merchant and Tacoma North End developer, built the Shore Line Railroad Company along Ruston Way in 1887, not only to compete with the Northern Pacific, but also to allow workers to commute from Old Tacoma to New Tacoma. The idea that Tacoma ought to have a municipal rail line first emerged in 1885, when Mason appeared before the Tacoma City Council and proposed the City establish mule- or horse-drawn trolleys on Pacific Avenue from downtown to Old Tacoma. But he was unsuccessful. The City would not back his plan.

Mason was not easily dissuaded, however. For two years he unceasingly campaigned for his idea, sending a flurry of handwritten letters to city fathers and focusing his powers of persuasion in face-to-face meetings. Mason's persistence eventually paid off. The city council finally approved plans for a Tacoma streetcar system, earning Mason the nickname, "Tacoma's Best Salesman." Local business leader Nelson Bennett walked away with a fifty-year franchise from the City to operate it.

Bennett knew railroading. He and his brother had successfully engineered and directed construction of the Stampede Pass Tunnel through the Cascades. With Mason as a trustee, the Tacoma Street Railway Company officially rumbled to life on January 19, 1887.

It wasn't a smooth ride. Although he had hoped to start by June, Bennett's franchise agreement barred steam engines, which were supposedly too noisy, even though they were less expensive than their electric counterparts and faster than horses. Preserving the environs for a pricier and less effective compromise is a proposition that sounds familiar even to this day.

The project immediately fell behind. Undaunted, Bennett and Mason appealed to the City. With money committed and rail ties on order, seven long months passed before Mayor Ira Town, on August 19, 1887, approved a second, less restrictive franchise.

Even this didn't expedite matters. In fact, the delay renewed debate as to whether it would be horses that would win the day for Tacoma rail—or horsepower. At long last, on May 30, 1888, a horse-drawn Tacoma Railway car ambled down Pacific Avenue to McCarver Street in Old Tacoma, its 14-passenger, bright yellow cars (with upholstered seats) turning heads left and right.

ENTER, AND EXIT, THE OPPORTUNISTS

With Bennett's franchise underway, the council soon awarded four more franchises before Bennett's line was even built. Energetic *Daily Ledger* editor and ex-*San Francisco Chronicle* man Randolph Foster Radebaugh and prominent business leaders George Franklin Orchard, Eben Pierce, and Albert A. Honey also entered the streetcar business. Other visionaries included George W. Thompson, Horatio C. Clements, James O. Carr, Frank C. Ross, and Fred E. Sander, to name a few.

Bennett also knew market competition. While the council was still awarding franchises, Bennett upgraded his system to electric trolleys. He even went further, acquiring cars and essential equipment from the Sprague Electric Railway and Motor Company of New York. Promptly thereafter, Bennett then sold the Tacoma Street Railway Company to a group headed by newspaper and railroad magnate Henry Villard, "the railroad Napoleon of the '70-'80 period," according to *Hunt's History of Tacoma* and an international figure in railroad development.

COOK'S FOLLY: TAKE THE EL

One bright summer day in 1892, curious, distinguished visitors and potential investors gathered at the Tacoma Post Office building at 1016 Pacific Avenue to examine a display of an entirely new type of urban transport solution: an elevated, electric-powered railway. Lucian Ford Cook, a Tacoma real estate dealer and inventor, was the man behind this ambitious project.

According to an 1893 article in *Street Railway Review,* Cook had already spent 12 years on the concept. His model included two narrow tracks, one above the other, suspended from poles on a single line of piers. Cook designed the car to be suspended from the upper track and stabilized by horizontal wheels at the bottom of the car, bearing weight against the lower rail. This light, narrow car, only three feet wide, could carry between eight and thirty passengers, all seated in single file.

The article confirmed that Cook received two patents associated with his idea. The first: "Elevated Friction Cable Railway - Lucian F Cook, Tacoma, Wash - No. 496,188 - Comprises a car hanging from an upper track, and a line of friction drive wheels acting against said cars to move the same, mechanism whereby said wheels are driven, consisting of conical or inclined drums carried by said wheels, the pitch or inclination of said friction drums, and that of the drive drums being different, whereby a wedge shape space is formed between said parts, and a travelling cable supported by said friction drums and drive wheel drums."

The second: "Elevated Railway System - Lucian F Cook, Tacoma, Wash - No. 496,189 - Combines in a system of elevated railway propulsion a car suspended off its center of gravity with a traction rail having an inclined tread portion and a drive wheel on said car having a correspondingly inclined tread."

Cook estimated a cost of $15,000 a mile (about $380,000 in today's money) to construct a route from Tacoma's Commencement Bay to Seattle's Elliott Bay, a trip that he thought would take about 20 minutes. Eventually, he found enough support to build a full-sized model about a quarter-mile long on the waterfront below the Tacoma Hotel, which stood on A Street between 10th and 11th Streets.

Using this model, railmen conducted test runs on the afternoon of Friday, November 26, 1892. Empty-car tests went so well that as many as 10 riders at a time volunteered for the "manned" tests to follow, but they proved to be a less-than-stable experience.

Chief Civil Engineer Henry Shaw, who also served as the project's motorman, said he would not be afraid to run a train at 100 miles per hour. The great Puget Sound historian Murray Morgan wrote in 1995 that Cook, believing his creation could top out at 200 mph, "spoke of the possibility of a transcontinental train that would deliver the New York morning papers to Tacoma at 1 p.m." It was stuff straight out of a Jules Verne novel.

However, the Panic of 1893 struck a few months later, and gone went the investors, their money—and Cook's intriguing idea.

From its January 17, 1910, obituary of Lucian F. Cook, the *Tacoma Daily News* wrote: "[While Cook] felt the stress of the panic of 1893, he never lost faith in Tacoma. He was extensively engaged in operating a line of steamers on the Sound in the early '90s. His active and resourceful brain prompted him to engage in many enterprises, one of which was the invention of a railroad operating on an overhanging rail. He erected an extensive model on the Northern Pacific ground south of the 11th Street Bridge, and while its feasibility was pretty thoroughly demonstrated, he was not able to interest the capital required to put the system into operation."

Sadly, this inability to raise the necessary cash—brought about by a nationwide financial panic beyond his control—means that we will never know what an elevated suspended high-speed train could have meant for Tacoma, but it is not hard to imagine that its impact could have been profound.

Special thanks to Paul Curtiss for his assistance.

Villard owned the Oregon Railroad and Navigation Company. A former newspaper reporter, he had a clear understanding of power and news making. In a previous bid to make Portland the western U.S. hub for the transcontinental railroads, Villard had bought his way onto the Northern Pacific Board of Directors (serving for a time as its president) and had nearly succeeded in gaining total control of the Northern Pacific, a move which would have resulted in the railroad being diverted from Puget Sound.

Meanwhile, Bennett, by getting out while he was still ahead, secured the rarest of status in Tacoma rail's mostly profit-free history. He made money.

With a massive $500,000 equipment budget, not to mention the old Bennett franchise's exclusive rights to some of the city's busiest streets, Villard's new Tacoma Railway & Motor Company in 1890 became the town's first electric streetcar system. With 11 cars rolling on the city's streets by March that year, city politicians and business leaders were energized by their local economy's growth potential.

Villard's chief competitors included the Radebaugh brothers' Wapato Park Belt Line Railway Company, which laid rails from Tacoma to points many miles distant; Judge Fremont Campbell's Tacoma Central Street Railway Company, later sold to the Union Pacific; and the Point Defiance Railway Company, owned and financed by one Allen Mason, the man who'd started the whole streetcar dream in this town some five years earlier when he had stood before the council, pleading for them to share his vision.

An early streetcar, #27 operated by the Tacoma Railway and Motor Company, was photographed around 1893 posed next to a treeless Wright Park. The car was part of the 6th Avenue streetcar line which ended in Glendale, a residential development located near 6th and Proctor. Tacoma was booming. As residential areas were developed far from the city core, available transportation was a major selling point. Several small streetcar lines were started, but by 1898 all of the smaller lines were bankrupt. By 1899, they were consolidated into the Tacoma Railway & Power Company. *Courtesy Tacoma Public Library, G66.2-020*

Villard was in it to win and three months after it began carrying passengers, his company added 32 new cars and extended service. From the edge of town, riders could now catch trains to Steilacoom, Puyallup, American Lake, and Seattle. But this competitive edge was soon dulled.

Following the Panic of 1893, real estate values plummeted, along with the value of many of the streetcar lines that were already living on borrowed financial time. When markets eventually corrected, even the big fish in the pond such as Villard had suffered. While Tacoma Railway & Motor Company had acquired a few smaller, troubled players—those with potential—foreclosures doomed other lines. In better times, the move to pick up some of the smaller street railways might have paid dividends; now it only succeeded in weakening Villard's company.

TACOMA RAILWAY & POWER COMPANY

Sure enough, emerging from the morass just before the turn of the century were the Pacific Traction Company (which in spite of its name was based in Maine) and the Tacoma Company of New Jersey (the progenitor of the Tacoma Municipal Belt Line Railway). Eastern business interests gained control of all the street railway lines operating in and around Tacoma. Both of these companies eventually fell under the control and ownership of the New Jersey-based Puget Sound Electric Railway Company.

In December 1898, representatives of three local railway companies (the Tacoma Traction Company, the City Park Railway Company, and the Tacoma Railways Company) agreed to form the Tacoma Railway & Power Company—a "street railway for the workingman." One could argue this was the moment Tacoma Rail was born, as this was the merger of companies from which the Tacoma Municipal Belt Line would originate.

Behind $2 million in capital stock and a bond issue of another $1.5 million, the three owners of these smaller street railway companies took control of Tacoma's street rail network. Now the city offered riders one unified system of routes.

CONNECTING THE TIDEFLATS

With the financial panic over, jobs once again plentiful, and an 1898 Yukon gold strike prompting migration into the region, Tacoma experienced yet another growth spurt. From 1900 to 1910 its population increased, from just under 38,000 inhabitants to 83,743.

By 1912, streetcar routes covered most of Tacoma with one exception: the Tideflats. Virtually inaccessible to streetcar traffic at the time, the Tideflats were, however, reached by two national railways—the Northern Pacific and Union Pacific—which maintained service to the handful of industries there.

Easily the largest obstacle to those streetcar companies aspiring to reach the Tideflats was the cost to traverse the 11th Street Bridge. A city ordinance required any street railway operating over the structure to pay a toll for its upkeep: ten cents per car—steep in those days. Although the Tacoma Railway & Power Company probably could have afforded to pay, it took an alternative approach instead. To extend service to the Tideflats industries, the company developed a route reaching the area from the south, rather than from 11th Street.

Streetcar routes covered most of Tacoma, but to reach the Tideflats riders had to cross the bridge on foot. Finally in February 1914, the City placed rail across the 11th Street Bridge (now the Murray Morgan Bridge), shown in this 1947 image. *Courtesy Tacoma Public Library, D25736 TPL4491*

For a decade, Tacoma Railway & Power Company passengers reached the Tideflats by getting off the Pacific Avenue line at the 11th Street Bridge, crossing the bridge on foot, and then boarding another line on St. Paul Avenue. But now with Tacoma's economy on the rise, that impractical "ride-walk-ride" approach to reach the Tideflats demanded a more convenient solution. With its thousand-strong workforce in freight car repair shops, the Milwaukee Road (and other Tideflats entities) generated, on paper at least, enough need for a streetcar system into the flats.

Someone was going to have to step up and assume the risk and responsibility. Asked by the City to operate a 24-hour line over the bridge, the Tacoma Railway & Power Company wanted no part of the operation. Pleading with them to return, the City lost more time, as well as two ballot initiatives, to raise street rail cash. Tacoma Railway & Power Company estimated a price of $87,000 (or about $2 million in today's money) to erect a mile and a quarter of single track, buy a transformer and four streetcars, and erect a car barn. Finally in February 1914, Tacoma agreed to install a line across the 11th Street Bridge, which would be operated by Tacoma Railway & Power Company using its cars.

OTHER PEOPLE'S MONEY

On January 10, 1915, an electric trolley loaded with dignitaries, including Mayor William Seymour, navigated the shiny new, mile-and-a-quarter Tideflat line. When the line officially opened to the public the next day, a thousand riders came on board.

But winter soon gave way to spring. When laborers could resume walking to work, they did just that. Down $4,000 by its first birthday, the line was struggling just to recover its investment. This became a long-term fiscal weight around the neck of Tacoma Railway & Power.

With war now raging in Europe, 1916 saw the arrival in Tacoma of three major shipbuilders and the Drydock and Shipbuilding Corporation. Additionally, the Foundation and Seaborn companies were expected to bring in some 4,000 additional workers.

New shipyards rose and in the spring of 1917, the Tideflats surged with activity. When the United States entered the war, the Emergency Fleet Corporation, the construction arm of the United States Shipping Board, stepped in to provide builder incentives and aided in the finance of the Todd yards, designating monies for the building of barracks to house one thousand workers and advancing the city money to extend the municipal Belt Line along 11th Street. Todd's Tacoma yard built Cascade-type freighters. These were 380-foot, 7,500 dead-weight ton steel ships.

In April 1915, the Tacoma Publicity Committee sponsored a race from Tacoma to the mountain (in Ashford), pitting a train against four automobiles. The Milwaukee Special beat the closest motorcar by five minutes. *Courtesy Tacoma Public Library, TPL1039*

Christening the USS *Omaha* at Todd Shipyards in Tacoma on December 14, 1920, are Louise Bushnell White with (order unknown) C. W. Wiley of Seattle, president of Todd Drydocks Inc.; William H. Todd of New York City, president Todd Shipyards Corporation (believed to be at left); and J. A. Eves of Tacoma, vice president and general manager of Todd Drydock and Construction Corporation. The *Omaha* was the longest vessel to be launched in the Northwest (at 550 feet, 6 inches) and the first ever to be launched bow first. It was a scout cruiser, the first of 10 scheduled to be built for the U.S. Navy, three then under construction at Todd. The *Omaha* (CL4) was built as Hull #30 and was delivered to the U.S. Navy on February 24, 1923. *Courtesy Tacoma Public Library, B3345*

During this period Tacoma also struck informal agreements between the four national railways to haul freight at night: log cars ran into the mills and steel was delivered to ship builders. The then-rare use of the rails after nightfall saved time, reduced congestion, and helped boost civic confidence regarding the eventual profitability of train service. It was the beginning of freight revenue dominating any other kind of moneymaking on the Tacoma tracks.

In May 1917, six weeks after the United States declared war on Germany, the City took over responsibility for the extension to the Todd and Foundation shipyards—2½ miles of rail, plus ten new cars. The council approved a $180,000 utility bond issue, but owing to the street railway's weak finances, not a single one of the area banks wanted in.

Unfazed, the council directed the City's electrical utility, Tacoma City Light, to purchase the entire bond issue (and a 25-year Pierce County operating franchise) with money from its general fund, effectively "robbing Peter to pay Paul." This, too, was a practice that continued in ensuing years. (Some could argue this was the moment Tacoma assumed real municipal ownership for the next century.)

To construct a wooden trestle over the Milwaukee Road shops into the shipyards by the target date of October 1, 1917, a crew of 110 began working 10 hours a day, including Sundays. The good news: Commissioner of Public

THE TACOMA STREETCAR DISASTER

Independence Day 1900 began with rain in Tacoma. Men, women, and children jammed themselves shoulder to shoulder on both the front and rear platforms of Tacoma Railway & Power Company trolley car No. 116. The crowd, headed to the downtown Independence Day parade, spilled out onto the running boards as they clung to outside railings.

The streetcar, filled to well over capacity, rolled down the long Delin Street Grade and headed into a left curve onto the "C" trestle. The car rapidly gained downhill momentum, causing the motorman, F. L. Boehm, to brake near the bottom of the grade at 26th Street.

The car's speed picked up, and Boehm, alarmed, released the brake and reversed the motor, which he believed would slow it down. But instead, the fuse blew, leaving the car without electrical power. Now fearing the worst, Boehm quickly reset the brakes and applied sand to the tracks, but to no avail. Moving at least 30 miles per hour, the car careened into the tight left-hand curve. It jumped the tracks and cleared the trestle's foot-high guardrail, plunging 100 feet into a steep ravine and landing upside down amidst several felled trees and a shallow stream. The *New York Times* later wrote, "The car jumped the track and was smashed to kindling wood in the bottom of a chasm over a hundred feet below."

People many blocks away could hear the wreck. Help arrived quickly, but the twisted wreckage and deep ravine hampered rescue efforts. Tacoma police and fire personnel, as well as doctors and nurses from nearby hospitals, rushed to the scene and began removing the injured and dead to a nearby city pumping station.

It was one of the nation's worst streetcar accidents. Forty-three people died, and many more were injured. What should have been a day of celebration had turned into one of tragedy. Boehm (who had three years' motorman experience but had only been on the Tacoma job for a few weeks) broke both his legs in the crash. His conductor, J. D. Calhoun, died.

A coroner's inquiry panel spent three days investigating the accident. Streetcar experts testified that when cornering, the car should have been traveling slower than 10 miles per hour, with the brakes off. Too much braking, combined with excessive speed in a curve, causes the brake to hold the rail too rigidly, possibly leading to derailment. This was precisely what Boehm had done.

Ten days later, the inquest laid official responsibility on the Tacoma Railway & Power Company. Human error on the part of motorman F. L. Boehm was also cited. In the ensuing flurry of legal actions filed against it for injury or wrongful death, the Tacoma Railway & Power Company nearly went bankrupt. Ultimately the company put more than $100,000 (approximately $2.5 million today) into a trust fund and informed the lawyers to receive the money and distribute it among the claimants; otherwise, the railway would go into receivership. With no other viable choice, the lawyers accepted the settlement.

On Independence Day 1900 what should have been a day of celebration turned into one of tragedy. An overcrowded trolley jumped the tracks, plunging 100 feet into Tacoma Gulch, killing 43 and injuring many more. An inquest laid official responsibility on the Tacoma Railway & Power Company, charging driver error had caused the accident. Shown is the aftermath of the accident. *Courtesy Tacoma Public Library, GM004*

Works Charles D. Atkins was able to secure streetcars for a low price, procuring from Salt Lake City four electric streetcars, four trailers, and a 240-horsepower electric locomotive capable of pulling 15 cars.

The bad news: Atkins missed the October 1 deadline. On that day, the Milwaukee railroad viaduct was not yet completed. Unperturbed, Mayor Angelo V. Fawcett held the line's maiden run anyway. "Two cars, with glossy paint of orange and black, made the first official run over the new Tideflats extension line . . . with the mayor as conductor on one," said a *Tacoma Ledger* report of the event.

PORT OF TACOMA'S BIRTH

In 1911, the Washington State Legislature passed the Port District Act, which enabled counties to establish public port districts. By this time, the waterfront of Tacoma had become a hive of activity—with lumber, wheat, and coal cargo traffic, as well as pleasure craft and ferry boats.

The Tacoma Chamber of Commerce commissioned an engineer by the name of Virgil Bogue to create a development plan for the Commencement Bay waterfront. Inclusive of touristic ideas as well, the Bogue plan zeroed in on the Tideflats: "With her enormous area of Tideflats, which reach all the way up to Puyallup and beyond, with the courage and help of her people, Tacoma will become one of the great ports. Without that courage and help, development will at best be slow and uncertain."

In 1914, county politicians decided it was time for citizens to vote to create a port district and commission. But, according to Murray and Rosa Morgan's 1984 history, *South on the Sound: An Illustrated History of Tacoma and Pierce County*, "the plan subsided into a swamp of citizens' committee studies, never to reappear."

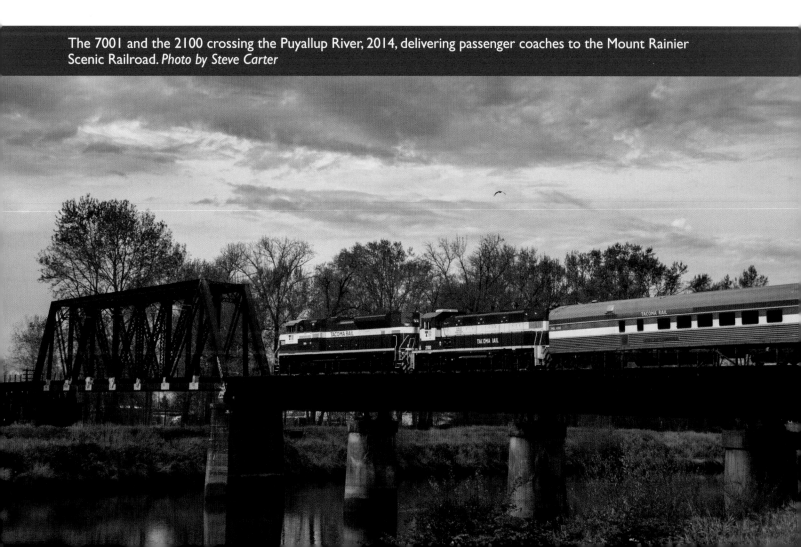

The 7001 and the 2100 crossing the Puyallup River, 2014, delivering passenger coaches to the Mount Rainier Scenic Railroad. *Photo by Steve Carter*

Crossing the Milwaukee Trestle on the way back to the yard, 2006. *Photo by Steve Carter*

Public opinion in the county precincts initially was strongly against spending money on a port district. After the United States entered World War I in 1917, demand surged but labor was scarce. Then, in the election of November 1918, the proposition creating the publicly owned Port of Tacoma passed overwhelmingly. Voters installed longshoreman Edward Kloss, farmer Charles W. Orton, and banker Chester Thorne as port commissioners.

The Port of Tacoma officially opened on March 25, 1921. On that day, the development of the Port and the Belt Line became linked.

GROWING PAINS AND DISHONESTY

Back on dry land, streetcar demand rose and riders outnumbered seats. Adopting an honors system for its five-cent fare because it could not afford to hire additional car personnel to collect, the city nicknamed its street railway "the honest man's car line."

Ironically the City of Tacoma soon exited the business of running the street railway. Mere days after the launch of the Tideflats line, the council opted to reopen negotiations with Tacoma Railway & Power Company, hoping to lure it back into public-private partnership.

The result was a two-year deal under which the City promised to furnish the streetcars and pledged to hold TR&P harmless from "fire, strikes and lockouts, faulty construction and 'Acts of God.'" Meanwhile Tacoma Railway furnished conductors and barns.

The 7002 leads a heavy train across the Milwaukee trestle, 2014. *Photo by Steve Carter*

As the Great War intensified, so did demand for ships. The closing weeks of 1917 saw a wave of thousands more ship laborers descend on the area—far above the railway's passenger capacity. Even with all 18 cars in use, the street railway could safely handle only about 4,000 riders a day—just a third of the now 12,000 men working in the Tideflats.

Many riders hopped cars any way they could—pushing and shoving into the trolleys, hanging off car roofs and out windows—and ignored the fare. So much for "the honest man." Serious injuries were commonplace, and in one particularly gruesome accident a switching engine killed a Todd worker. As 1917 came to a close, the railway had racked up a financial loss of $7,400. This was no way to run a railroad.

When Tacoma Railway & Power begged for help the following year, the City made a feeble effort to purchase the company for $6.5 million, only to be soundly rebuked by the voting public. The City took it up the line, appealing in a nine-page detail to its recent friend the Emergency Fleet Corporation for a $1 million loan. They answered to the tune of $232,400 (adjusted for inflation, about $3.6 million in 2015), money it stipulated for double tracking the existing line, adding new cars, and building a "pre-pay" station at South 10th Street.

Thus began a flow of federal cash earmarked specifically for Tacoma street rail. In October of 1918, the City took in a first installment of $50,000 of EFC money. The occasion also marked the unofficial end of the line for the Tacoma Railway & Power Company's partnership with the City. The Tideflats street rail's net loss of $13,725 in 1918 proved too much for Tacoma Railway & Power, and they canceled their contract with the City.

THE CITY TAKES OVER

Taking over the operation of all freight and transit from Tacoma Railway & Power, the City of Tacoma and Commissioner of Public Works H. Roy Harrison named Joseph H. Lyons as general superintendent of transportation on the Tacoma Municipal Railway on January 1, 1919. According to the announcement of his appointment to the post, Lyons, the former secretary of the Citizens Street Railway Advisory Committee, was "widely known among labor union men of the coast." The superintendent's job was actually split that first year. W. G. Denny, the Tacoma Railway & Power master mechanic, left that post to become superintendent of power and equipment. In ill health, however, Denny resigned his post in late 1919.

With Tacoma now in the motorman's seat, the street line went out and hired 100 able-bodied men to fill the vacated Tacoma Railway & Power roles. The transfer of ownership brought hope.

It didn't last long. The promised line double tracking, along with a new South 10th Street station, fell far behind schedule. The end of the war meant shipyard jobs were disappearing, along with the funds to pay those able-bodied City employees.

When streetcar motors fell into disrepair, the City returned to the Emergency Fleet Corporation trough, scoring an additional $36,000 to buy ten new motors. In 1919 alone, Tacoma ran up a tab of $72,000 on the street railway. Tacoma would be hard-pressed to recoup these funds, without its moneymen resorting to the raiding of various other municipal coffers to pay down its passenger rail debt—thus the origin of the Tacoma Rail pejorative phrase, "the stepchild utility."

Although it had been designed to be self-supporting, the muni was already in trouble. Neither Public Works Chief Harrison nor Arthur Carlson, a former line inspector who had succeeded W. G. Denny as rail superintendent, could do much to improve its finances or service the overloading direct-current generator powering the rail line's deteriorating infrastructure. In 1922, the city finance commissioner, Jesse Silver, assumed control of the railway, forcing out Superintendent Carlson in favor of his brother-in-law, Andrew Gunderson.

No question about it, running a streetcar company—or even a single streetcar—profitably in a city like Tacoma was extremely difficult. While the local economy rose and fell with the war effort, which benefited the streetcar operators for a time, demand simply didn't last.

The streetcar era expired relatively quickly. By the late 1930s, the last remaining trolleys gave way to buses, which were more versatile and cheaper to maintain. Belt Line buses hauled passengers for the last time in 1946. But the train *tracks* remained, and on Tacoma's industrial Tideflats, the short-line Tacoma Municipal Belt Line Railway emerged.

In the new age of the bus, the streetcar proved by comparison a fleeting, cumbersome, and costly mode of transport. The Belt Line, until 1925 known as the Tacoma Municipal Street Railway, was the city's last streetcar line, and it remains the city's sole link to its days of electric trolleys and conductors. But the rail's freight-switching operation, always the railroad's mainstay, continues. The switching railroad on the Tideflats has a history every bit as colorful as the city it serves.

The newly acquired SD70 ACe-P4s poised and ready for service in Tacoma Rail's main yard, 2014. *Photo by Steve Carter*

One of the first DPU Mode (distributed power) trains to Frederickson with the SD70 ACe locomotives, 2015. *Photo by Steve Carter*

The GP40 4001 leads the Train to Trek along the shore of Lake Kapowsin on its return from Eatonville to Tacoma in the fall of 2008.

Power duo. The SD70s with Josh Banks, manager of operating practices and safety, standing at the top with Greg Seifert II, conductor, at bottom.

Aerial image taken in 1947 of Buffelen Lumber Company on the Tideflats. A long-time customer of the belt line and Tacoma Rail, the company made doors, plywood, and other specialty wood products. products. Although no longer rail-served, the company is still a going concern. *Courtesy Tacoma Public Library, B284453.4*

FOR THE LONG HAUL

CHAPTER FOUR

With the honors system failing, the railway's passenger operation was surely going bankrupt. However, in an otherwise dismal mix of good intentions and dire fiscal consequences, the freight-switching arm of the municipal line was breaking even.

Perhaps freight could be the answer.

Between 1918 and 1919, switching revenues topped $41,000. What had begun largely as an afterthought—a supplement to the passenger line—now looked like a promising source of revenue and growth. And indeed, just four years hence, the City was switching and spotting cars, at $5 per, from all four national carriers: the Northern Pacific, Oregon-Washington, Great Northern, and the Milwaukee Road.

It was a sometimes-bizarre arrangement. The same line that was running trolleys in the morning began also to accommodate freight switching after the evening passenger rush. But with no rail yard, no double tracking, and only makeshift sidings, trolleys often stood in the way of the switching locomotives. Motormen simply found an out-of-the-way place to park after hours, clearing the tracks for freight cars.

Freight switching grew in fits and starts. While some work came in, such as log hauling into the Buffelen Lumber Mill on Taylor Way, revenues were still not steady enough to make a significant dent in the situation. Eventually, if it meant alleviating some of the crippling rail debt, the City of Tacoma found it was not above begging for debt forgiveness. It had the audacity to ask the Emergency Fleet Corporation to forgive the $200,000-plus loan it granted the City back in 1918. The Emergency Fleet Corporation's reaction? It sued the City.

When Tideflats development began anew in the early 1920s, the City and Pierce County ratified an agreement to lay track across the Hylebos Waterway to East Side Drive County Road and place more switching operations at the east end of the Tideflats. By August 1923, Tacoma's street railway, crippled financially and also facing the Emergency Fleet Corporation lawsuit, had to confront the bleak vision of obsolescence at the hands of the national trunk railroads. It was not a pretty picture.

There had to be a way to generate enough cash flow to service the heavy debt load and improve the service.

DOLGE AND McCUNE

The Ernest Dolge Inc. sawmill, located on Taylor Way on the Belt Line, occupied 16 acres on the Hylebos Waterway. The sawmill and its 55 workers produced timbers used in boat construction and for house beams and sold high-grade lumber nationwide for fire ladders.

In addition to owning one of the largest mills in the Tideflats, Ernest Dolge served as chairman of the Tacoma Chamber of Commerce Transport Committee in the 1920s and president of the Tacoma Lumbermen's Club, which focused on bringing logging activity, new customers, and industries to the area. He was on the record in lumber trade journals as being concerned about creating (or losing) savings in freight, citing in the *Lumber Manufacturer and Dealer* "slow delivery and much dissatisfaction" as his chief concerns.

Minneapolis-born Jay W. McCune served as secretary on the Tacoma Chamber of Commerce Transport Committee under Dolge. McCune, a Spanish-American war veteran who had driven trucks for the Northern Pacific and had also worked for St. Paul and Tacoma Lumber, worked for 38 years heading up the chamber's traffic and transportation efforts. He played a vital role in rail and shipping matters, the development of Tacoma roads and bridges, education, and more.

So Dolge and McCune, one a mill owner with a side specialty in transportation and the other a promoter of Tacoma with professional transport expertise, became the "right place at the right time" local business leaders interested in steering rail's development. These smart, motivated, and well-connected businessmen understood the economic potential of freight switching in the Tideflats.

The pair was just what Tacoma rail needed, and neither was about to let the opportunity pass. Dolge had recently been in New Orleans, where the City owned a belt line that performed switching for industries, the New Orleans Public Belt Railroad. (Tacoma Rail and the New Orleans Public Belt Railroad are among only twelve publicly held short line railroads left in the country, according to the American Short Line and Regional Railroad Association.) Having seen the future, he returned to Tacoma, eager to persuade an unenthused Mayor Angelo Fawcett. The way Dolge viewed it, the municipal switching operation was a subject all too often overlooked by the city council.

He resolved to change all that.

BIG RAIL ENTERS—GIVING BIRTH TO THE BELT LINE

The fates were about to become even kinder toward rail in the city.

Over the next four months, Dolge and McCune met with the other major railroads serving the Pacific Northwest. The response they received was tepid until October 1923, when Charles Donnelly, president of the Northern Pacific at the time, paid a visit to the Tacoma Chamber.

Back in March 1922, Donnelly had assured Dolge and fellow mill owner John Buffelen rail facilities for Tacoma mills. Dolge and McCune rolled out the red carpet upon one of Donnelly's visits. They also helped orchestrate a *Tacoma Daily Ledger* editorial touting a municipal Belt Line and calling for the cooperation of the major railroads, which hit the newsstands just as Donnelly arrived.

Donnelly was sold. The Northern Pacific was all in, he said. The move to use the municipal line for switching brought a tremendous response from Tideflats industries and shippers, in turn compelling the Great Northern, the Milwaukee, and the Union Pacific to pony up for access themselves. Suddenly, any industry located in the Tideflats had direct, inexpensive access to each of the four transcontinental lines.

Pictured in 1927 (left to right) are Charles Donnelly, Northern Pacific; Ralph Budd, Great Northern; H. E. Bryam, Chicago, Milwaukee and St. Paul; and Carl R. Gray, Union Pacific. Donnelly's approval of switching Northern Pacific trains in the Tideflats in turn compelled the Great Northern, the Milwaukee, and the Union Pacific to enter, accelerating the birth of the Tacoma Municipal Belt Line. *Courtesy Tacoma Public Library, G44.1 061*

Four unidentified men gaze at a line of railroad flatcars stacked with mahogany logs on May 1, 1925. Bound for the Buffelen Lumber and Manufacturing Company, the cargo, a product of the Philippines, had arrived at the Port of Tacoma on the "Wheatland Montana." The arrival of the logs marked a transition to direct transactions between the overseas grower and a Tacoma manufacturer. Prior to this, mahogany used in fine furniture, cabinets, and other purposes was brought here in board form. *Courtesy Tacoma Public Library, B12440*

All four players gained access to municipal tracks and promised uniform switching service. The municipal railway performed all switching duties for a flat, $3 per-car switching fee. The national railroads charged a two-step rate in addition to the Belt Line's fare, based on the cargo destination. The carriers settled on a three-level fee schedule. Shipments from one Tideflats industry to another (also known as "inter-terminal") cost $5.55 per car; hauls outside the Tideflats were $8.50. Lumber companies paid $2.50 per car for log hauling.

After two years of negotiations, on October 29, 1924, Dolge, McCune, Mayor Fawcett, and representatives from all four railroads signed a contract giving them access to municipal track in return for uniform switching service from the Belt Line. Despite the fact Buffelen protested the signing, claiming the Milwaukee was not paying an equal amount for cost-sharing on its end of the log-car switching negotiations, the Belt Line was born.

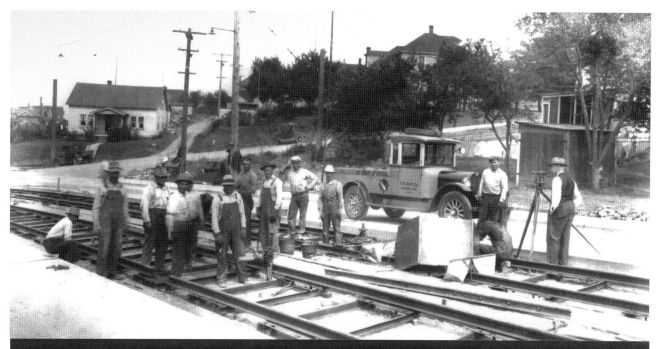

In July of 1930, this gang of Tacoma Railway & Power Company employees was laying new streetcar tracks on Delin Street, just north of Holy Rosary Church between Tacoma Avenue and Fawcett. One of the workmen is crouched behind a metal shield labeled "danger." The man at the far right is standing behind a surveyor's level. The house at the left is believed to be 2909 Fawcett. Less then ten years after this photo was taken, Tacoma's streetcars were no longer running, and Tacoma was in the process of ripping out its tracks and selling the metal for scrap. *Courtesy Tacoma Public Library, B22763*

HIGH POINTS, LOW DEBT

It was a high point to be certain, and the *Daily Ledger* commented: "Tacoma takes rank as one of the few industrial centers of the United States and the only one in the Pacific Northwest to have a large industrial district served by a Belt Line railroad." Realizing its potential impact on the future of the city, the newspaper continued: "The full import is not fully apprehended by the layman . . . [but the agreement] will have a great influence in the future development of the Tacoma tideflat district."

More glad tidings: at roughly the same time, the municipal railway's debts were finally about to shrink. Tacoma's city council paid the Emergency Fleet Corporation an out-of-court settlement of $115,000, not only canceling the railway's obligation to the City's general fund, but also eliminating its gross earnings tax. This was very welcome relief.

Unquestionably, developments were at last moving in the right direction. In 1925, the first full year of Belt Line service, the freight-switching service nearly doubled its revenues to $54,373, and the street railway posted its first net profit under municipal ownership. Also, Dolge and McCune suggested the name of the street railway be changed formally to the Tacoma Municipal Belt Line Railway (TMBL), a moniker that lasted until 1998.

Dolge's well-timed energies advanced rail in Tacoma precisely when and where the city needed it most. "Patron saint" or opportunist, he ultimately was a man who simply ran a business and wanted access to rail transport. Any way one looks at it, however, Ernest Dolge can justifiably be remembered as the father of the Tacoma (Municipal) Belt Line.

On Wednesday, December 30, 1925, at 7:55 p.m., a municipal streetcar crashed through the steel gate that closed off 11th Street when the bridge was raised. The *Virginia V*, docked near the bridge, sped to the rescue, pulling survivors to safety, including four who were injured. The death toll reached five. Pictured (l to r) are *Virginia V* crew members David Balduzi, Alfred Jergenson, Captain Nels G. Christensen (at back), J. Christensen, Joe Brooks, Claude Williams, and Al Torgeson. *Courtesy Tacoma Public Library, G50.1-062"*

DISASTER AND DEBT

At 7:55 p.m. on Wednesday, December 30, 1925, a municipal streetcar crashed through the steel gate that normally closed off 11th Street whenever the drawbridge was raised. The wooden car barreled through a pair of barricades, plummeting into the icy water below, breaking apart and spilling passengers as it fell. Five passengers died.

The crew of the *Virginia V*, a ship docked near the bridge, witnessed the wreck and sped to the rescue, pulling survivors to safety. Despite their efforts, only four people, including motorman Clyde Staley, survived. Staley was later found guilty of "failing to exercise reasonable precaution in the handling of the car." The fatal incident was costly. Although it thankfully did not approach the magnitude of the 1900 street railway tragedy, it nevertheless was the Belt Line's worst accident in terms of lives lost, and it left the railroad accountable for $40,000 in damages and legal fees.

Then came disaster number two. On Sunday afternoon, June 24, 1928, a fire quickly spread in the Tacoma Municipal Belt Line's main car barn, located at 11th Street and Taylor Way. A three-alarm event, according to the *Tacoma News Tribune*, the spectacular blaze drew hundreds of onlookers. The entire barn burned down to the ground; the fire destroying all but two of the city's 24 streetcars—$276,000 worth. Inexplicably, none were insured. Foul play was suspected, as the disaster took place during a period of labor-management tension. But no wrongdoing was ever proven.

On December 30, 1925, a municipal streetcar crashed through the steel gate that normally closed off 11th Street whenever the drawbridge was raised. Five people drowned. *Courtesy Tacoma Public Library, B16995 TPL1426*

In the aftermath of the fire, the Tacoma Municipal Belt Line initially leased a few cars from the Tacoma Railway & Power Company. Control of this decision was under Public Utilities Commissioner Ira S. Davisson (already overseeing Tacoma's Light and Water Utilities Divisions), who quickly moved to buy seven secondhand streetcars from the Perry-Baxter-Doane Company of Boston for $30,100.

"Secondhand" is perhaps too generous a term. On delivery in February of 1929, the cars were in such disrepair they required substantial renovation of their motors, upgrading from coal burning to electric heating, and even refurbished wheels. Eventually, however, these cars became rail-worthy and were some of the last trolleys that ran on Tacoma street rails.

A third, lesser fire in 1929 (for a time taking out of service the Milwaukee viaduct at 11th Street) was noteworthy in that, in its aftermath, employees demanded alternate transportation. Bus service was established until the trestle could be rebuilt. The buses were quick, clean, and efficient and proved a harbinger of the demise of Tacoma street rail.

Grown accustomed to operating in debt, the Belt Line still owed City Light an eye-popping $348,000. Twin 1930 analyses, one by a "Belt Line commission" of Tideflats businessmen including Dolge and McCune and the other by city council members, left behind a singular impression: the primary function the municipal rail line served was clearly not to generate revenues (much less profits), but rather to lure industry to the city. It thus played a role as a valuable economic engine, even if it failed to make money.

This insight proved wise. Freight switching was on the rise. Freight-car pulls for 1931 totaled 13,500, shooting up to nearly 20,000 by 1938. On the other hand, passenger traffic steadily declined. Fleet size told the tale: whereas there had been 38 streetcars rolling in 1920, by 1930 only nine remained. It was becoming more and more clear that the days of Tacoma's passenger streetcars were numbered.

The #66 streetcar, full of passengers, was hitched up to two "nags" and driven up Pacific Avenue on June 9, 1938, at noon to promote the huge "Last Ride" celebration planned for June 11. Tacoma's last streetcar had been taken out of service in April of 1938; the cars replaced with city buses. *Courtesy Tacoma Public Library*

GET ON THE BUS

It was time for Tacoma to catch the bus.

As difficult as it was to deal with the continuous decrease in its passenger traffic, the belt line managed to survive, thanks in no small way to Belt Line Superintendent Charles H. McEachron. Just 33 years old when he took over the job from Andrew Gunderson in 1926, McEachron was the first Belt Line chief to establish some accountability for the organization. Over his 14 years at the helm, McEachron helped ease the transition to buses, expand the Belt Line's passenger service to the Eastern Tideflats, and acquire the line's first and only steam engine.

McEachron made plans in 1936 to purchase 21 new buses. The plan was to phase in buses and end streetcar passenger service altogether, before eventual conversion of the entire Belt Line trolley. So in 1937, the company set up a one-year trial, putting three distinctive Yellow Truck and Coach Company buses into service, bought from this Chicago-based subsidiary of General Motors.

During the late 1930s, freight switching increased Tacoma Municipal Belt Line's momentum, with the railway handling up to 150 cars per day. Adding switching power, McEachron purchased a steam locomotive (Tacoma Municipal Belt Line's first and, as it turned out, last steam locomotive) from the Northern Pacific for $1,000. By May of 1938, with the arrival of six new White Company buses, the streetcar era in the Tideflats was over.

The first of 85 new buses emerge from a boxcar in this February 1938 image. By replacing the streetcar system with buses bought from the Twin Coach Company of Kent, Ohio, the City of Tacoma would exit the passenger market, handing over that business to Tacoma Transit Company (now Pierce Transit) on January 1, 1947. *Courtesy Tacoma Public Library, A7071-1*

During WWII, Tacoma faced a shortage of city buses. Pictured (l to r) are Tacoma Utilities Commissioner Robert D. O'Neil; Amos Booth, the Belt Line superintendent; and Walter Frankland, local transportation administrator, who had coordinated the U.S. Navy lease of eight diesel-electric buses. *Courtesy Tacoma Public Library, D13931-1*

McEachron's time at the railway was over shortly after. In 1940, new Utilities Commissioner Bob O'Neil thanked McEachron for his services. His legacy included rallying the Belt Line from the tragedies of the 1920s and successfully guiding a debt-ridden entity while also managing to increase freight switching and improving the value of the rail service. Themes challenging the next two superintendents, Amos Booth and Neil Kime, included a wartime bus controversy, freight logistics and infrastructure, and the recurring Belt Line nemesis—debt.

TURMOIL AND ACHIEVEMENT

Overall, the 1930s marked an upturn for the line, with freight leading the way to a 1935 annual net profit of $2,668, the organization's first bottom-line use of black ink instead of red. At the end of the decade, the war in Europe had brought increased industrial activity to the Tideflats, and with it, a flood of shipyard workers.

Although the new Belt Line chief, Amos Booth, had led the city's sanitation department as superintendent, when it came to the rail business he had zero experience. But he did possess a unique qualification: he had helped Utilities Commissioner O'Neil win election to that post. Booth's apparent reward for his service was running his very own Belt Line railroad, warts and all.

With a war on, and Tacoma shipyards open for business, the city experienced yet another population boom. From its 1940 census total of 109,000 citizens, Tacoma grew to more than 143,000 in 1950. By winter 1940, huge increases in shipyard workers strained the limited passenger capacity of transit into the Tideflats. Soon Booth saw his company overwhelmed by demand and hampered by an acute nationwide bus shortage. Forced to scrounge wherever possible for secondhand vehicles (not to mention cash), Booth and the line tried their best. However, a number of issues plagued Booth's administration: exorbitant expenses, fluctuations in the number of workers in the Tideflats, constant equipment breakdowns, and finally, the desperate employment of refurbished buses that had originally been used at the New York World's Fair—which were vastly oversized for Tacoma's streets and proved to be dangerous traffic hazards.

In March 1942, the Tacoma Municipal Belt Line became an official railroad in the eyes of the Interstate Commerce Commission (ICC), subject to provisions of the Railroad Retirement Act of 1937. Under the regulation, Tacoma Municipal Belt Line retroactively owed freight-switching workers retirement and unemployment benefits totaling $27,500—money it simply didn't have. Again, Tacoma Municipal Belt Line was forced to borrow—this time it borrowed from City Light, and despite transporting a record 150,000 passengers a month, it still continued to lose money. Cliff Erdahl, who had succeeded O'Neil as utilities commissioner, investigated the never-ending losses and came to the conclusion that offering passenger service was a "march in the wrong direction." Tacoma Chamber of Commerce Transport Committee agreed. It seemed only a matter of time before the City would exit municipal passenger operation altogether.

And yet there were bright spots. Freight traffic soared. During World War II, Todd Pacific Shipyards built 74 warships and employed more than 30,000 Tideflats workers. With several new industrial customers, the line's switching locomotives were now pulling up to 350 cars a day, which also led to the addition of new track. In 1944, Amos Booth decided to drop 100 percent of the electric locomotives in favor of diesel-electric.

A modest fee increase instituted with a new freight-switching agreement with the carriers in 1943 helped bring about the major achievement of Booth's term: construction of the Milwaukee Way Interchange Yard, a modern freight-switching yard built on 15 acres at the end of the Sitcum Waterway near 11th Street and North Sitcum Avenue. Booth secured part of the needed funding from a $128,000 Federal Works Agency grant and an additional $50,000 federal loan. And he plunked down $101,000 of the Belt Line's own resources.

November 1957: Massive storage tanks at Kaiser Aluminum dwarf the Canadian National Railway boxcars standing alongside. From 1947 until its bankruptcy in 2000, Kaiser was a long-time Tacoma Rail customer, occupying a ninety-six-acre site. *Courtesy Tacoma Public Library, A109978-2*

Commissioner Erdahl asked for Booth's resignation in February 1945, just a few months before the new yard opened. Booth's departure as chief must have been bittersweet. The bus mess had been his, and now the Belt Line was climbing out of its freight infrastructure woes

FORWARD PROGRESS

Neil Kime, the Belt Line's next boss, arrived from the Tacoma office of the State Tax Commission, having helped manage the county auditor's office and the Veterans of Foreign Wars. Thus Kime brought extensive managerial know-how (although no prior rail experience) at a time when the Belt Line desperately needed a financial healer. He was more than up to the challenge. First, the City exited the passenger market, handing over that business to Tacoma Transit Company (now Pierce Transit) on January 1, 1947. Next he improved the power, moving the railway out of the electric era permanently when he added four diesel locomotives over the next few years (including a pair of 65-ton, 590-horsepower, Whitcomb diesel-electric engines in 1947).

Whether it was Kime's leadership or the sheer unburdening of the long-time Tacoma Municipal Belt Line obligation to passenger service, the organization was for the first time in good financial health. By 1952, the Belt Line was switching 82,000 cars per year, and switching revenues had risen from $29,000 in 1947 to $55,000 in 1952.

Kime acquired additional track along Lincoln Avenue from the Northern Pacific and expanded the Milwaukee Way yard to hold more cars. Freight volumes rose steadily, and freight revenues helped erase many of the debts Booth had incurred during the scramble to add buses during World War II. Beginning in 1947, net revenues shifted the annual income statement into the black for the first time in years, an achievement that prompted the city council to praise the company's management in writing. From a 1948 resolution: "For the first time in 32 years the Belt Line is a modern, first class railway equipped to adequately take care of the industrial area it serves without financial loss to the City of Tacoma."

Kind though they were, those words did little to improve the Belt Line's harsh twin realities of long-term debt and aging infrastructure. Its stated purpose as an "industry lure" aside, the Belt Line had accumulated thirty years and counting of red ink. And though it was the 1950s, the line was still operating on World War I rails. Equipment and facilities were out of date; locomotives in ill repair. Meanwhile, revenues and rates remained soft. Something needed to be done.

The switching rates the national railroads paid Tacoma Municipal Belt Line were never quite enough to offset expenses. Trunk lines felt this switching railroad shouldn't earn a profit—after all it was a government entity. The result: instead of devoting extra revenues to much-needed upgrades, whatever meager profits Tacoma Municipal Belt Line did earn went directly to City Light and other creditors.

Despite occasional renegotiation with the big railroad customers, Tacoma Municipal Belt Line rates were insufficient to turn the tide for the rail line. To make ends meet, Tacoma Municipal Belt Line deferred maintenance and took on still more debt—locked in a dismal cycle of minimal to non-existent maintenance, aging facilities, and spiraling operating costs.

RAIL SUPERINTENDENTS IN TACOMA

1919: Joseph Lyons

1919: W. G. Denny

1919–1922: Arthur Carlson

1922–1926: Andrew Gunderson

1926–1940: Charles McEachron

1940–1945: Amos Booth

1945–1958: Neil Kime

1958–1964: Carroll Burks

1964–1976: Donald Carlson

1976–1979: Jack Kanan

1979–2005: Dennis Dean

2006–2008: Paula Henry

2008 (Interim): Alan Hardy

2008–Present : Dale King

"Past and Prologue?" – Tacoma Rail Terminal Superintendent Tim Flood (left) discusses his philosophy of precision railroading with former Superintendent Dennis Dean (right) at the centennial open house celebration in August 2014.

DEBT FREE

Amazingly, Tacoma Municipal Belt Line's downward debt spiral was about to end when Tacoma's revised 1953 charter changed it to a city-manager form of government (and along with it, the job of Tacoma Municipal Belt Line superintendent changed from a political appointee to a hired employee). In one fell swoop, the City of Tacoma wiped out the long-time debt owed to City Light.

It was a stunning reversal of fortune—thirty-five years of debt erased. What a deal!

The year 1956 saw the first of many times to come that the City would consider an arrangement to improve the Port of Tacoma's efficiency by adding Tacoma Municipal Belt Line to the Port, pricing it for potential sale to the Port, or otherwise increasing that rail-port connection. The initial idea didn't get far, however. The Public Utility Board authorized a 1958 rate increase instead.

In April 1958, Neil Kime concluded his 13-year run. In spite of the Belt Line's "one step forward, two steps back" revenue model, Kime's administration had made capital improvements and had enjoyed annual growth rates never before seen. Taking with him a favorite catchphrase, "The Belt Line is not as long as other railroads, but just as wide," Kime had left it in better shape than he'd found it, handing the superintendent role to a lifelong railroader, Carroll P. Burks.

RATE AND TURF WARS

Burks had worked with the Pennsylvania Railroad and later with U.S. Army rail operations during World War II. He had also supervised building a railroad in Liberia. Determined to keep Tacoma Municipal Belt Line solvent and running with greater efficiency, his almost immediate attempt to have the trunk lines pick up a hefty 22 percent increase in switching rates was roundly rejected by the four major carriers. The carriers, which held all the power in the negotiation, countered with an offer to buy Tacoma Municipal Belt Line.

Burks and his bosses knew this move would not have been in Tacoma's best economic-growth interest. Private rather than public ownership would mean dramatically higher switching costs, the risk of fewer customers, and the loss of some $25,000 per year the Belt Line paid in taxes into the City's general fund.

In March 1959, trunk line representatives backed off on the acquisition idea, instead proposing (and getting) a measly 5 percent switching increase, well under Burks's originally proposed 22 percent rate hike. Unhappy with the insufficient increase, Burks asked for another hike within a year. When the major carriers resisted, Public Utility Board member Ernest K. Murray, a former city attorney in the earliest days of street rail who himself wanted Tacoma out of the municipal rail business, threatened to force the issue by filing a tariff with the Interstate Commerce Commission. Although the idea didn't fly, it would return in a slightly different form a quarter century later. But this was February 1960 and the four carriers responded with a 10 percent hike proposal, again proposing to buy the Belt Line from the City.

What a luxury for the client to set the price! The Public Utility Board refused, countering with a 15 percent rate increase. Another year passed and after intense negotiation, all parties reached a compromised 8.36 percent retroactive fee increase.

A few more years went by and suddenly the City was looking to sell Tacoma Municipal Belt Line—but only to the Port of Tacoma. Short of cash in 1962, the Public Utility Board set a price of $317,000 (about $2.45 million today) for exclusive purchase by the Port.

The idea made some operational sense, and it came with the backing of the council and the Tacoma Chamber of Commerce. It appeared the Port was going to get the railroad, but a time-consuming process to arrive at a ballot referendum was required. Despite efforts by City Manager Dave Rowlands to rush a city council discussion onto the agenda, the proposed port acquisition of TMBL never made it to the November 1962 ballot. Needing more time for legal due diligence than was available, the City retained the rail line.

This pattern repeated itself. The Port periodically became interested in buying the railway, asking the railway administration to stay on as operator. Each time a deal drew close, however, either the Port or city councilors, hoping to engineer an ownership switch, balked when faced with significantly increasing rail-switching fees to make such an agreement possible. While the port and rail operations were in proximity, they really did have vastly different missions.

In 1963 the Belt Line showed improvement, with gross revenue at $497,374, up $61,806. Its net was $68,075—up a whopping $40,781.

In 1964 when the Port was planning its industrial waterway, the Port Commission offered to pay for a new Belt Line headquarters and relocate it from its old Taylor Way location to a new yard and headquarters on East-West Road. The waterway extension was designed to replace the Belt Line on a new circular route around the entire area, opening more of the Tideflats for customers to set up operations. Since this new rail facility and classification yard construction was already going to cost the taxpayer $1.1 million, once again the city council proposed selling Tacoma's rail to the Port. The deal died after Councilman Dick Haley convinced a majority of his colleagues that the Port's offer was insufficient.

Economics kept the railway municipal. As a city entity, the Belt Line was paid by the major railroad clients and not by the shippers who negotiated their rates with the main rail lines themselves. (As a subcontractor to the main lines, the Belt Line's rates didn't get back to the shipper.) Selling the railroad would have been shortsighted, a one-shot financial boost for the city, with no future revenue.

In July 1969, the new TMBL headquarters and classification yard opened for business. Built for $909,000, the long-overdue switching facility was capable of handling 440 cars and designed to expand well beyond that number.

This 1979 image provides a look at the Tacoma Municipal Belt Line fleet, featuring the 900s and, on the far left, the 1200. When intermodal shipping arrived, the Belt Line didn't yet have large locomotives. It used individual, 1,000-horsepower switching engines such as the Alco-built 921, a design dated to the 1940s. The locomotives Tacoma Rail uses today can be configured up to 4,300-horsepower.

After six and a half years on the job, Carroll Burks was lured away to become president of the American Short Line Railroad Association. His tenure had its ups and downs. The Belt Line gained switching power with the 1964 addition of a 1950, one hundred-ton diesel locomotive, but they still owed City Light for the 1944 Milwaukee Way yard construction. Growth was slow, long-term debt remained, and money for improvements remained non-existent.

NEW MAN, NEW ERA

The new rail chief, Donald E. Carlson, ushered in a new era. A former assistant superintendent on the Northern Pacific, Carlson brought with him operating knowledge. Without the distraction of Port sale rumors, he inherited a better situation than his predecessor.

Carlson purchased two relatively larger locomotives in 1967—a pair of 1950s vintage, one hundred-ton, 660-horsepower Alco engines that cost $9,000 apiece. The Alcos weren't fast, but they could pull. The rails they ran on were a different story, however. Derailments caused by track failure were becoming a daily occurrence.

In July 1969, the new Tacoma Municipal Belt Line headquarters and classification yard opened for business. Built for $909,000, the long-overdue switching facility was capable of holding 440 cars and was designed to expand well beyond that number. Still, maintenance, renewal, and capital replacement programs were non-existent. Well-intentioned efforts to better serve customers brought operational setbacks, such as track deterioration and a lack of inspections.

During the 1970s, log hauling elevated Tacoma Municipal Belt Line carload totals to new highs. In 1971, Tacoma Municipal Belt Line began hauling its first automobiles, for Toyota. Net incomes rose in modest increments to record levels in 1972. Revenue exceeded $1 million for the first time in 1973. As money arrived, so it went out. Expenses jumped to all-time highs due to soaring fuel prices, and higher taxes ate away at the bottom line.

In December 1971, Carlson initiated a program to repair and in some cases rebuild rail, much of which had been in place since the 1930s. Carlson brought in Jack W. Kanan, a former Northern Pacific roadmaster he had worked with both in World War II and on the narrow gauge Alaskan White Pass and Yukon, to oversee the task of rebuilding 33 miles of Tacoma Municipal Belt Line track. Talk about tax dollars at work: the program proceeded piecemeal through the entire decade of the 1970s and on into the 1980s. Also participating in the project was 34-year-old Dennis Dean, who would later serve as the Tacoma Municipal Belt Line superintendent throughout the 1980s and until December 2005.

Eventually, Don Carlson grew tired of the lethargic progress of the railroad. He chose early retirement at age 59 in 1976. Despite inflationary woes and an energy crisis, Carlson had guided Tacoma Municipal Belt Line through a more or less stable, if financially dim, four years.

ENTER KANAN

After only four months as acting superintendent, Jack Kanan stepped up to the superintendent's role. Helping to bring the Belt Line into the modern era, Kanan adopted a 24-hour operating schedule. The railroad now had its classification yard, its new headquarters at 2601 SR 509 North Frontage Road, and thanks to Kanan's old friend Don Carlson, four 1,000-horsepower, 115-ton diesel locomotives purchased between 1971 and 1976.

Facility upgrades aside, 60 years of existence hadn't changed much in the overarching story of the Tacoma Municipal Belt Line. Money remained a struggle. During those inflationary times, the Belt Line barely broke even and logged several consecutive years with annual operating incomes in only five figures. Tacoma Municipal Belt Line in the late 1970s saw modest gains in improved volumes and earnings. But years of deferred maintenance left track and facilities in poor condition, negating most perceptions of progress.

Kanan was a hard taskmaster. His relentless effort to hold people accountable earned him the nickname, "Canine," and reports hold that workers unhappy with his tough management style spray-painted mocking "K9" graffiti on switch targets in the yard. While Kanan was resourceful at procuring essential material for Tacoma Municipal Belt Line, what the line really needed was a strong influx of dollars to rebuild the railroad from the ground up—but this was outside his control.

Under Kanan, revenues perked up, which enabled the addition of an elevated yardmaster's tower and the purchase of a 1,200-horsepower GM Electro-Motive diesel (EMD) locomotive (No. 1200) in 1978. It's also worth noting that with No. 1200 came the safety-minded introduction of a red-and-white color scheme, still in use today at Tacoma Rail.

MOMENT OF TRUTH

Overshadowing whatever problems existed at the Belt Line, as the 1980s dawned, the U.S. freight industry was on the brink of ruin. Decades of regulation and intense competition from trucking and barges had reshaped shipping. Rail's share of the pie had dwindled to 35 percent of the market, down from 75 percent in the 1920s. Making matters worse, poor infrastructure slowed whatever rail commerce there was.

With the Northern Pacific having already been absorbed into Burlington Northern in the 1970s, only the Union Pacific and the Burlington Northern remained from the original four Tacoma trunk line customers. Weyerhaeuser began running on the former Milwaukee Road as Chehalis Western.

The Milwaukee Road declared bankruptcy in 1977. One positive side effect of the Milwaukee Road's demise was a number of its employees turned to Tacoma Municipal Belt Line for employment. Many were younger workers, but even with just nine or ten years of railroad experience, they brought with them a level of professionalism and a camaraderie that continues to help shape the internal culture and overall atmosphere of Tacoma Rail today. For an ex-Milwaukeean, coming to Tacoma Municipal Belt Line felt familial and offered a railroader the benefit of working on the railroad all day and sleeping in his own bed every night.

The view from inside the tower, circa 1999, featuring Steve Barkhoff (left) and then yard clerk Dave Riggers (behind).

The operations control tower after receiving a facelift in the winter of 2015.

Jack Kanan retired in September 1979. Helped by a 13 percent per railcar rate increase with the big carriers that had gone into effect the previous summer, his legacy was one of financial solvency, despite Tacoma Municipal Belt Line's truly horrid infrastructure. However, in other ways Kanan's time had reflected a low moment for the Belt Line. The company was plagued with unsafe rail and hampered by uncertainty in contracts with the major railroads. TBML had no extra money for upgrades and, even though it was soon to add younger Milwaukee Road people, an aging workforce.

Carrying the burden of change isn't easy and Kanan had not been well liked by the employees of the Belt Line. Morale worsened when rumors again flew regarding a possible Port of Tacoma takeover bid. The railroad had arrived at an important junction. Would it choose renewal or face continued decay?

A nice back-to-back look at the 4002 and the 1524 in 2011.

The 1521 dressed up during the 2005 holidays.

TR 1521 delivering to Pabco, alongside an unusually empty SIM yard, 2015. *Photo by Steve Carter*

TR 1521 spotting a tank car along Port of Tacoma Road, 2015. *Photo by Steve Carter*

The new 2200 eco units haul the excursion train during the 2012 Tacoma Rail Open House.

Look what's at the end
of this Rainbow, 2015.
Photo by Steve Carter

RAILROAD RENAISSANCE

In an about-face from the excessive federal regulation of the past, in 1980 Congress passed the Staggers Rail Act. The legislation eliminated many damaging regulations that had hindered competitive, efficient, cost-effective freight rail service.

History shows the Staggers Act sparked a renaissance in U.S. railroading. Freight lines became profitable. Short line and regional railroads, most of which developed since Staggers, revitalized the industry. Today the short lines and regional railroads operate some 45,000 miles of track in 49 states, and as of 2014, they employ approximately 18,000 people.

Dennis Dean arrived as the right man at the right time as superintendent for the Tacoma Municipal Belt Line. During Dean's time at Tacoma Municipal Belt Line (1977–2005), exponential growth became possible, and its rebirth set the stage for the emergence of the modern-day Tacoma Rail. In sum, the Port of Tacoma rail operations merger occurred.

The railroad's workload transitioned from decades of commercial servicing of warehouses, chemical plants, and the like to supporting port-based, international assignments and intermodal customers. Tacoma Municipal Belt Line changed its identity and expanded its horizons through its operating agreement with the City of Tacoma's Department of Public Works to run the City's recently acquired Mountain Division.

A former Burlington Northern assistant yardmaster who had worked for Kanan, Dean started at Northern Pacific in 1958 and had most recently worked as an assistant general yardmaster for Burlington

Dennis Dean served as superintendent from 1979 until 2005. The era Dean presided over saw tremendous expansion, and he established the solid foundation that remains beneath Tacoma Rail to this day.

Northern. He had joined the Belt Line as the assistant superintendent in 1977, having already worked nearly 20 years in rail with stops at the Northern Pacific, Milwaukee Road, and Burlington Northern. His father had been an influential career man with the Northern Pacific, serving as an agent and later as director of security.

Dean always viewed his job as one of stewardship. Tacoma's municipal railroad was an asset to the city and its customer base, and he saw his role as maximizing its value. Straightforward and tough in labor negotiations, Dean knew every job on the railroad and ran it as he saw fit. One night, Tacoma Municipal Belt Line needed portable electrical power to enable emergency maintenance. At the time, Dean knew City Light kept some 26 portable generators on hand. Shortly after his urgent request for one was denied, Dean had heated conversations with both Light Superintendent James E. Thompson and Utilities Director Aldo Benedetti, letting each man know he and TMBL would never again be treated that way.

The first decade of Dean's tenure was a constant battle for financial support and firmer political footing. Utilities Director Benedetti had hired Dean. Soon after Benedetti's successor, Paul Nolan, appointed Dean to TMBL's top post, the railroad would become embroiled in yet another potential Port of Tacoma takeover of Belt Line operations.

SURVEY WARS

Tacoma pioneered the on-dock rail system with the 1981 opening of the North Intermodal Yard (also known as NIM), the first dockside rail yard on the West Coast. Inefficiencies plagued the rail setup inside the Port. Cargo mismanagement could, and often did, result in significant delay during the elaborate, multi-movement exchange from trunk line to Belt Line to port to industry.

During the winter of 1981, the Port hired the engineering consulting firm Tippetts Abbett McCarthy Stratton, who projected the coming intermodal wave. They recommended a port upgrade, spending upwards of $173 million over twenty years to remain competitive. The report also suggested the Port take over the Belt Line to improve performance.

Dean's response was to conduct his own analysis. The STV/Management Consultants Group he brought in took a look that spring and determined the Belt Line outperformed the port railroad in five of six measured categories. Citing Tacoma Municipal Belt Line's superior experience, the feasibility study recommended consolidation of port rail under Belt Line management. Port supervision would have brought standardized, time-efficient throughput, but Tacoma Municipal Belt Line remained the better-equipped entity—the specialist.

A 2004 aerial look at the North Intermodal Yard (foreground). *Courtesy Port of Tacoma*

Events overtook this latest scrape in the long history of strained Port of Tacoma-Belt Line relations when the Union Pacific briefly flirted with running directly into the port on the former Milwaukee rails. Bypassing the Belt Line would have substantially driven up switching fees and would have made life politically awkward for the UP, with the BN and Chehalis Western having to make up the difference in lost switching fees. Then United Grain, a major Tideflats customer and the critical player in UP's bypass plan, severely cut back its operations in 1982. The UP stayed on, but Tideflats revenues dropped for both the Port and TMBL.

TMBL grew nicely during Dean's early years as chief. Over time, Dean built and was able to execute five-year and 10-year plans while simultaneously securing trackage, operations, fleet upgrades, and building upgrades—all with inferior rates. "We fought within the utilities at the City for some leveling of the playing field, we fought with the carriers, and we fought with the Port of Tacoma who thought they wanted to be in the railroad business," Dean said. "We finally got rate increases, and I believe a lot of that groundwork was laid so that current staff can be given the support they need."

REBUILDING FROM THE RAILS UP

A pair of 1984 studies, one commissioned by Tacoma Municipal Belt Line and executed by Stoery Transportation Services (STS) and the other performed by the Federal Railroad Administration at Dean's request, uncovered plenty of problems in need of correction.

The report identified four hundred defects in 24 miles of track, ranging from missing bolts to cracked rails. Lowering rail speeds to 10 miles per hour and pushing hard to put new processes into place, from switching to safety to employee training, Dean saw this moment as the Belt Line's big opportunity. Tacoma Public Utilities management agreed, delivering much-needed upgrade funds of $1.6 million. But with its ancient infrastructure, Tacoma Municipal Belt Line remained stuck in the past until Dean put his foot down once and for all in 1985.

Dean's STS study recommended scrapping the Belt Line's antiquated 1950 rate in favor of a modern, independent, tariff-switching rate of $159 per car. Not surprisingly, when informed of this idea, the national railroads had zero incentive to go along with either the policy change or the proposed amount.

Preparing a Union Pacific train with Tacoma Rail power in 2011.

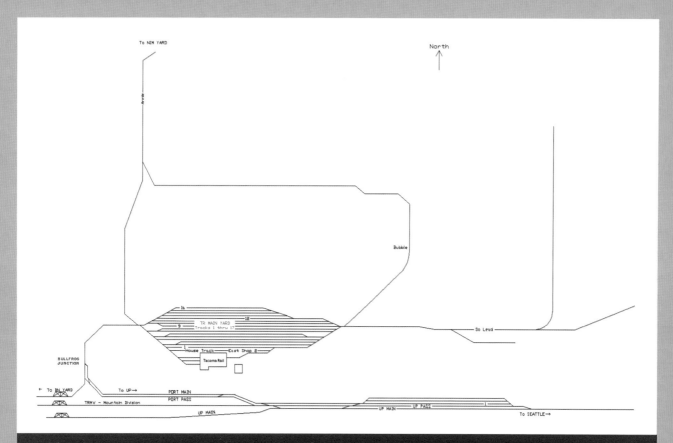

A 1980 schematic of the Tacoma Rail yards.

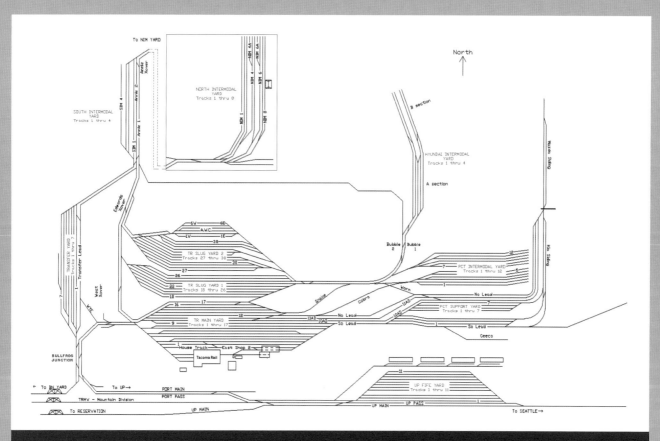

A 2014 look at the same land shows the 30-year evolution of track capacity.

So Dean, the Public Utility Board, and the Tacoma City Council simply canceled the contract, drafting and submitting a new tariff with the Interstate Commerce Commission. For Tacoma Municipal Belt Line this compromised, $77.45 per-car tariff led to a stable future. For the big carriers, it signaled a choice between absorbing new, higher rates or passing along the Belt Line's fees. They agreed to the new rates.

The tariff approach harkened back to an idea first floated by Public Utilities Board member Ernest K. Murray in the late 1950s. Early in his career, Murray had served as a city attorney for Tacoma and had actually presided over the 1925 inquiry into the streetcar incident on 11th Street. Murray had long been of the mind that Tacoma should either privatize its rail or divest. Flash forward to 1959. Murray nearly saw his wish become reality. When the trunk lines were harassing the City over Burks's big 22 percent rate increase proposal, Murray had had enough of the nickel and diming. He vigorously called for Tacoma Municipal Belt Line to end its dependence on the big carriers' prior approval by simply filing a tariff with the Interstate Commerce Commission and letting the markets decide.

Now, some 26 years later, Dennis Dean and his bosses were doing just that. On October 1, 1985, precisely 61 years after Mayor Fawcett had signed the first contract with major railroads, the Belt Line adopted the tariff and a new cost-of-service business model that gave it the ability to project revenues and expenses, reasonably forecast needs, and finally put some real distance between itself and financial uncertainty.

Until the tariff, Tacoma Municipal Belt Line rate or policy changes had to be justified through the carriers. Tacoma had been a stepchild for almost all of the trunk lines, except the Milwaukee—the only railroad that had a direct connection with the port. Everyone else had to come through the Belt Line. Before, rate policies had been under the control of the Union Pacific, the Northern Pacific, the Great Northern, and the Milwaukee.

The tariff changed all of that. Dean's move got everyone's attention, including that of the Burlington Northern, which became the next entity to briefly consider taking over the Belt Line. According to Jonas Simonis, terminal manager at then-Burlington Northern, until the tariff, Burlington Northern's upper management had never put any real value on the Belt Line, viewing it more as a necessary evil—the automatic addition of a 24-hour delay when shipping through Tacoma. "When a Belt Line acquisition was proposed to me, my answer was we couldn't do it well," said Simonis. "The Burlington Northern could not be as efficient as the Belt Line. Their crews are smaller, but if either of us said that we'll have the car up there and ready by this time, then it didn't matter what it was going to cost; it was a commitment."

According to Dean, whenever an interested entity—the Port or the Burlington Northern—was considering buying the Belt Line, their analysis of practices, procedures, rates, crew sizes, and costs signaled they couldn't do it as well or as cheaply. "That was our strength, and I believe that it's still relevant today," said Dean. "The fact remains that you have to provide very high customer service. Customers must feel a reliability that they can do what they do to make their money, without interruption. That's the driver."

The move to a tariff was gutsy, but it worked. Tacoma Municipal Belt Line got the rate increase that was politically allowed, giving it the ability to upgrade annually. Once it became cost-of-service funded, Tacoma Municipal Belt Line could generate the support it needed—meeting the ratepayer and setting agreements. The decision gave the Belt Line money to perform track repairs and purchase locomotives. The tariff made Tacoma Municipal Belt Line more reliable. It also synergized the relationship between the railroad and the Port of Tacoma, strengthening both.

THE PORT MERGER

On the heels of the tariff, and with the coming of the intermodal revolution and planned Port expansion, the Tacoma Public Utilities Board and the Tacoma City Council considered consolidating operations. Originally intended as a yearlong test, the 1985 merger of the Port's railroad and Tacoma Municipal Belt Line's operations wound up as a five-year trial. The catalyst for this undertaking was the relocation of Sea-Land Inc., a large steamship and container transport company, from Seattle to Tacoma.

The Port Commission and Utility Board drafted a memorandum of understanding dictating the terms of the trial. To service all intermodal customers, the port needed larger yard-switching capabilities. Under the deal, the Port took some track from the Belt Line and its old classification yard. In return they built four new tracks for the Belt Line at another location, including a second parallel track extending all the way from the Tacoma Municipal Belt Line yard to 11th Street.

Throughout Tacoma Municipal Belt Line's history there were always concerns that raising rates would undermine Tacoma's competitiveness against other West Coast ports. So while the merger was still in its trial phase, a consultant named Ron Ernst was brought in to assess logistics—analyzing time and motion

A straddle carrier (strad) stacks K-Line shipping containers at the Port of Tacoma's North Intermodal (NIM) Yard.

studies—and liaise between the Port of Tacoma, the Belt Line, and the major carriers. Working with the Belt Line during most of the trial timeframe, Ernst helped settle disputes and finalize the agreement.

Earlier in the decade, the Belt Line had begun 24-hour port rail operations, promising a 30-minute response time to port customers, thus allaying their concerns that the Belt Line might favor its own customers at the expense of the Port's customers.

Tacoma Rail mechanic Quang Nguyen makes minor running repairs to the MP1500 1521 in the locomotive servicing facility once affectionately known as the "Dean Barn" after former Superintendent Dennis Dean who oversaw its construction.

Trailer Train mechanics make repairs to a double-stack well car in preparation for its departure from the Pierce County Terminal (PCT) in the Port of Tacoma.

During the trial, operations were united and the various entities—the Burlington Northern, Union Pacific, and Chehalis Western—set daily meetings at the Port. For the next three years, a group numbering as many as 20 (and never less than six to eight) representatives planned daily operations, including train releases and steamship arrival schedules. Working together proved beneficial to all. According to Simonis, great trust developed and the partnering entities strengthened relationships as a result of this practice. "For a time, there was a move to create a control center in Tacoma that was manned by somebody from the trunk lines and the Belt Line and the Port, 24/7," he said. "Logistics and cost eventually got in the way, but the trunk lines realized the value of the daily meeting."

The trial continued until 1990, when the port railroad and the Belt Line entered into a permanent agreement, merging under an oversight committee made up of Port commissioners and Tacoma Utility Board members with the railroad operated by Tacoma Municipal Belt Line. For all those years they had co-existed at arm's length, partnership with the Port seemed more like an uphill battle to Tacoma Municipal Belt Line than collaboration. After all, the Port's primary goal with regard to anything occurring with the railroad was to keep rates low, a fact of life detrimental to rail's ability to stay fast and efficient. But the merger agreement, including a test period and a timeline, ushered out harsh feelings and brought in a new era of cooperation.

THE MOMENT ARRIVES

Tacoma Municipal Belt Line had reached a turning point. Port expansion provided Tacoma Municipal Belt Line the opportunity to view itself as something more than the little switching railroad it had always been. This was the moment the Belt Line finally "merged" with the Port of Tacoma and had the Port divest itself of the railroad. In the end, the Port saved millions, increasing its efficiency as it geared up for growth.

With the tariff in place and the merger complete, Dean returned his attention to infrastructure and finding the funds to upgrade it. Tacoma Municipal Belt Line was still running heavy, state-of-the-art locomotives and cars on rail that in a few remaining places dated all the way back to 1908. With a low-speed railroad, derailments might mean one or two wheels dropping on the ground; it wasn't life and death, but it did mean having to stop and re-rail. "For a long period, TMBL was unable to recover costs and there was great pressure to not allow us to recover our costs to the point where we could no longer build infrastructure to support our growing operations," said Dean. "That became more and more the responsibility of the Port."

After Utilities Director E. E. "Ted" Coates and Dean oversaw a comprehensive Belt Line inventory, they secured $250,000 by applying to the City's Capital Improvement Program for essential yard and track upgrades and new lighting in the classification yard. Combining those funds with a pair of loans, Dean initiated his 10-year upgrade plan and added two, 2,000-horsepower locomotives.

The Belt Line finally began to operate more independently, thanks to the improved rate structure and increasing access to financial resources. Annual revenues climbed. In 1991 the Belt Line took in $5.3 million on 60,071 cars switched. In a year they'd bumped that up to $6 million, despite the imminent termination of the logging activity (and switching). By 2000, the line's switching revenues rose to $8.1 million (up 53 percent compared to 1991) on 67,762 cars switched.

Through all kinds of weather, the 3001 appears clean and ready to roll.

Locomotive engineer Shelley George handles the first revenue move into break bulk terminal EB-1 in October 2014.

TACOMA RAIL
TACOMA PUBLIC UTILITIES

The moon rises over the yard office. *Photo by Steve Carter*

Working under the rainbow, 2006. *Photo by Steve Carter*

TACOMA RAIL
1521

TACOMA RAIL
2000

The 3801 handles commercial business on the Capital Division.
Photo by Steve Carter

ON THE FAST TRACK

CHAPTER SIX

The decade of the 1990s was like none other in the history of Tacoma's spirited train operation. The Chehalis Western logging contract ended in mid-1992, and the concurrent demise of logging—certainly not positive for the regional economy—delivered a significant psychological blow as well.

The timber industry peaked in 1965 and had been steadily declining since the mid-1980s. This decline was a result of three factors: reductions in timber harvesting from Pacific Northwest forests, changes in Asian demand, and the globalization of wood markets. Closer to home, the fallout over modernized, automated forestry and the fate of the northern spotted owl in the old-growth forests of the Pacific Northwest meant many above-average salaried timber jobs simply vanished, damaging regional economies and smaller, timber-dependent towns. What logging's demise really brought about, though, was the end of an era. Weyerhaeuser ceased its operation of the Chehalis Western, selling the Chehalis side for $3 million and the Morton side for the sum of one dollar to the City of Tacoma.

But it was not only the end of logging that posed a threat to the health of the region's rail businesses. Labor disputes also played a role. A strike in October 1992 by Tacoma clerical workers, including one Belt Line employee, lasted 15 days before union leaders accepted a new contract offer from the City. The 211-member Local 483 clerical unit went on strike after rejecting the City's offer of three percent pay raises in 1991 and '92 and cost-of-living-based raises in 1993 and '94. Union members had been working twenty-two months without a contract. They demanded far larger pay increases.

Reflective of the times, by the early nineties the original headquarters of the Tacoma Municipal Belt Line had fallen into a state of disrepair.

During the strike, about 1,100 city employees, mostly in the Utilities Division, walked off their jobs in support of the strikers. Rail crews returned to work after honoring the picket lines for the first eight days. Some city services were disrupted, including garbage and recycling pickup, service calls, and the Belt Line Railway at the Port of Tacoma.

When the conflict ended, the Port rail merger contract was amended in 1993 to include a clause allowing the Port to secure a third-party operator to provide rail service to the marine terminals —should a labor strike ever shut down the Belt Line again.

Interestingly, were another stoppage to hit, no assurances existed that the third-party carrier would ever have to relinquish those operating rights. This led to the very favorable contracts Tacoma Rail's operating crafts enjoyed until 2015. The "Death Sentence Amendment" was negotiated away in 2013 with the adoption of the new Port of Tacoma/Tacoma Rail Operating Agreement.

Mid-90s rail mergers—despite shrinking the number of overall carriers—signified the expansion of broad, coast-to-coast carrier networks. When Burlington Northern and Santa Fe joined in 1995 to form BNSF Railway, the prospect of a new and wider-ranging competitor compelled Union Pacific to follow suit. In 1996, it merged with Southern Pacific to form the new Union Pacific. While the competition meant fewer players, it also created two major carriers in the West in Burlington Northern Santa Fe and Union Pacific.

The Mountain Division resumed operation under the auspices of the newly branded Tacoma Rail in 1998 under City ownership through the Department of Public Works. The operating agreement between Public Works and Tacoma Rail has been extended five times, with the latest amendment running through December 31, 2016. It is the mutual desire of the City and Tacoma Public Utilities to arrive at a negotiated transfer of ownership of the Mountain Division to Tacoma Rail through a permanent sale of the property on terms favorable to all parties.

Switching activities resumed at a steady pace in 1999–2000, with the completion of new Hyundai port facilities (Washington United Terminals) in 1999 and a strengthening of the U.S. economy after the 1998 Asian economic downturn.

GRANTS

Toward mid-decade, switching activity began declining. U.S. and global economic constraints and the use of double-stack intermodal equipment (essentially a hybrid combination of a flatcar with a gondola, allowing for two stacked containers to pass most rail height restrictions) gave shippers significantly larger container throughput to increase shipping capacity. Greater container capacity meant fewer railcars were needed to handle the same freight volume.

One thing not on the wane during this timeframe was federal funding. Until the mid-1990s, grant monies available to rail hardly existed. Now Tacoma Municipal Belt Line seized the opportunity to secure available public money, becoming skillful at both sourcing as well as grant writing.

The railway received over $30 million from state and federal governments in the form of zero-interest loans and the occasional grant. Much of this success can be attributed to Dean's 1998 addition of Paula Henry as assistant superintendent. She excelled at grant writing and acquiring funds. State law at the time said the state money going out of the rail fund could only go to publicly owned rail entities. One of five in the state of Washington at that time, Tacoma Municipal Belt Line was by far the largest and most successful when it came to acquiring grants. Tacoma Municipal Belt Line began to acquire grant monies to upgrade ancient track and add or renovate facilities to keep up with intermodal traffic growth.

The Rail Division had never had access to funding to help it stay on top of its needs. When Paula Henry came onboard she endeavored to change that. Having worked previously for the former city manager and for the city's Water Division, she used her understanding of the ins and outs of governmental dynamics to help navigate a new course for TMBL.

Her efforts helped elevate the Belt Line's profile within the inner workings of Tacoma politics and proved influential, especially when Tacoma Municipal Belt Line was bringing the Mountain Division on line. "Together, they were kind of a mom and pop shop, where Paula and Dennis would play off each other, and it worked out really well," said Dan McCabe, current Tacoma Rail CIO and CFO, who began his Tacoma Rail career as a student contractor in 2000.

SHINY AND NEW

In June of 1998, the Tacoma Municipal Belt Line became Tacoma Rail. This rebranding came as Tacoma Public Utilities renamed its electric, rail, and water divisions, eliminating the government association. "We wanted to keep the TPU name, but we wanted to give the other divisions separate identities," Utilities Director Mark Crisson told the *News-Tribune*. Tacoma Power, Tacoma Water, and Tacoma Rail replaced Tacoma City Light, Tacoma City Water, and the Belt Line Railway.

Also that year, Tacoma Rail geared up for Hyundai with the purchase of a pair of rebuilt GP-20 diesel 2,000-horsepower locomotives, bought for $170,000 each from National Railway Chicago. The Tacoma Municipal Belt Line 2000 and 2001 units were the first Tacoma Rail locomotives equipped with dynamic braking, which uses a locomotive's traction motors to assist in slowing the train. "They were very heavy, and up until then we had never run big, heavy locomotives before," said Marc Robertson, current Tacoma Rail road foreman of engines, who at the time was a locomotive engineer. "Having only run switch engines, these new locos were the best we'd ever had up to that point."

The newly anointed rail line received ratification of a 1999 (biennial) budget of $19.6 million. Interestingly, in the legal sense, the organization to this day remains officially the Tacoma Municipal Belt Line Railway, doing business as Tacoma Rail.

HYUNDAI AND PORT PRESSURE

Hyundai's import activity brought major container traffic into its new Blair Waterway terminal. Hyundai expected to bring in around 100,000 containers per year, roughly half of which were loaded on special railcars bound for Midwest and East Coast markets.

In April 1999, the Port of Tacoma wanted to offer Hyundai a lower price for its services. With the permission of the Utility Board, the Port and Tacoma Rail put together a service package which would give Hyundai Merchant Marine a price break of as much as $300,000 off the cost of moving the shipping line's railcars around the Port.

This move was meant to offset an unusual pre-port and Tacoma Rail merger arrangement, where, beginning in December of 1999, Tacoma Rail charged $94 each for moving loaded railcars that originated north of East 11th Street and $155 for moving railcars originating south of it. Tacoma Rail agreed to roll back its rate to $89. But that rate reduction led to a loss in revenue that made it impossible for Tacoma Rail to pay

Mark Crisson, Tacoma Public Utilities director, inside a dome car section during the inaugural run of the Spirit of Washington Dinner Train in August 2007.

for the infrastructure the Port had built for it. "We had to go in front of City Council to reduce the rate for Hyundai," said Dean. "At the same time, we were trying to do our budget and establish a rate increase [for everyone else]."

Seeking improved efficiency of cargo movement, in late 1999 the Port of Tacoma also sought to create a special group to coordinate getting trains into and out of the port. This unified team made up of port, carrier, and rail operations people would act in a capacity similar to that of air traffic controllers—monitoring movements, expediting repair incidents, and planning ways to speed cargo containers as they moved from ship to railcar and eventually to transcontinental lines.

Dean and Tacoma Rail also began to address the need to build infrastructure to support the Port's expansion of marine terminals. To hold and process more railcars, construction began in 1999 on the Banana Slug Yards to support intermodal traffic growth in the North Intermodal Yard.

A Hyundai container in 2003. The Korean manufacturer's automobile import activity brought major traffic into the new Blair Waterway terminal in 1999. Hyundai expected to bring in around 100,000 containers per year, roughly half of which were loaded on special railcars bound for Midwest and East Coast markets.

Post Panamax gantry cranes at Washington United Terminal are backed by a well-maintained fleet of tractors, reach-stackers, side-loaders, and top-picks during intermodal cargo operations. A wholly owned subsidiary of Korean-based Hyundai Merchant Marine, WUT opened at the Port of Tacoma in 1999 and offers the shortest gateway from Asia and best protected harbor in Puget Sound. *Photo by Mick Klass*

A second such yard was built in 2001 for the Washington United Terminal and was later expanded by three tracks for Auto Warehousing Company. However, Auto Warehousing Company did not want to incur the cost as part of their facility development, so this yard became additional intermodal staging space. The 509 yard, as it is known, was built in support of the Pierce County Terminal in 2005. While a 1:1 ratio of staging track to terminal track was to be maintained, the 509 yard had been built in a location where intermodal rail switching was cumbersome. It fell short of the required staging-to-terminal track ratio. The concept was both the Pierce County Terminal and 509 yard tracks would be double-ended together going across Alexander Street, allowing the terminal to be serviced from the east end. As yet, this has not occurred.

In May 2009, the first intermodal train to run out of the North Intermodal Yard with distributed power (DP)—three locomotives on the head end and this single unit pushing on the rear end of the train.

Tacoma Rail agreed to lump all intermodal business together, establishing the effective rate of $89 per car. That was increased on December 18, 1999, to $94. Other traffic went up $10 ($145 to $155). Another $5 increase was implemented January 1, 2001, for both sets of traffic. At this point Tacoma Rail sought to raise rates (+$23) to adequately fund the Port of Tacoma's loan, but the Port objected to the increase. The loan was forgiven and the Port retained ownership of the Banana Slug Yards to keep the rail rates down.

Two former auto-loading facilities for Kia and Mazda were combined into one new complex in 2003, operated by Auto Warehousing Company, located adjacent to the recently finished Slug Yards.

GREGORIAN ODOMETER TURNS OVER

As the new millennium dawned, Tacoma Rail saw an explosion in intermodal switching, necessitating a round of hiring and asset acquisition. With 67,762 cars switched—the highest level since 1979—Tacoma Rail's 2000 operating revenues rose 17 percent or just under $1.3 million.

That was the good news. The bad news was the cost of switching service to intermodal that same year topped the additional $1.3 million in fees collected, resulting in a net loss for Tacoma Rail of $395,000. Then came an economic recession, and by 2001 the railroad's hopes for more hiring and expansion ended abruptly.

With Dean and Henry now adept at identifying and securing grant monies for developmental projects such as the Train to the Mountain (an "if you build it, they will come" approach), the more pressing spending need was in the Tidelands Division. Although no one could know it yet, the Mountain Division was soon to be encumbered by grant obligations of more than $30 million.

THE MOUNTAIN DIVISION

On May 5, 2000, Tacoma Rail announced the signing of a tentative agreement with the City of Tacoma's Department of Public Works to operate the Mountain Division (with the rail reporting mark of "TRMW"), the former Milwaukee Road line heading 13 miles up the road to Frederickson. Tacoma Rail now connected directly into Spanaway Lumber, a subsidiary of Oregon's TreeSource Industries. To mark the occasion, three passenger cars were coupled to a Tacoma Rail diesel locomotive to transport several dozen visitors to Frederickson and the Spanaway mill, where lumber was loaded directly onto trains, not trucks, for delivery to customers in the Midwest and East.

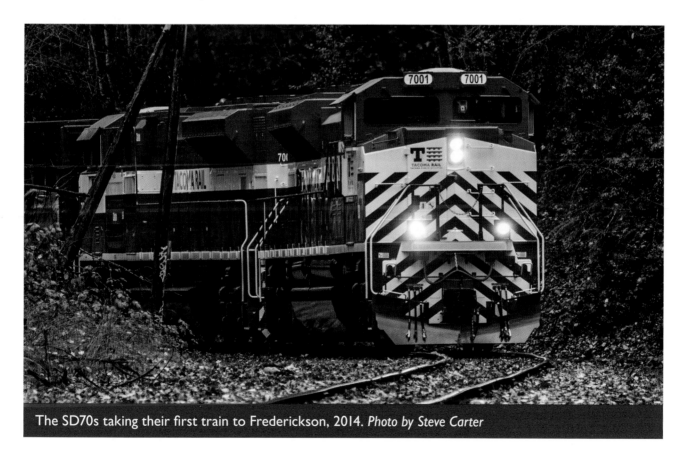

The SD70s taking their first train to Frederickson, 2014. *Photo by Steve Carter*

A 2014 look at the steepest part of Tacoma Gulch, 3.65 percent. A compensated grade for about two miles coming down, Tacoma Gulch presents a locomotive engineer with an immediate, technical, and downright nasty challenge. That grade starts with a table where a 204-ton diesel locomotive starts out, drops down, flattens out, and then goes over a hill in an almost rollercoaster fashion. The route then presents a pair of big S-curves and at the bottom a sixteen-degree curve set at ten miles an hour—and includes a stop signal. *Photo by Steve Carter*

Back in 1919, the Milwaukee Road took control of the Tacoma Eastern line, running it for the next 60 years. Weyerhaeuser purchased the line in 1980 and operated it as the Chehalis Western, moving mainly export logs to the port until the service ended in 1992. In 1995, the City of Tacoma bought the line to promote economic development. Under the purview of Tacoma Public Works, Tacoma Rail started operating the line in 1998 and renamed it the Tacoma Rail Mountain Division after the 3.3 percent grade up the Tacoma Gulch.

A compensated grade for about two miles coming down, Tacoma Gulch presents a locomotive engineer with an immediate technical challenge—and one which is downright nasty. That grade starts with a table where a 204-ton diesel locomotive starts out, drops down, flattens out, and then goes over a hill in an almost rollercoaster fashion. The route then presents a pair of big S-curves and at the bottom a sixteen-degree curve set at ten miles per hour—which also includes a stop signal. The main part of this line runs between Tacoma Rail's yard and Frederickson, where the railway serves an industrial park. The Mountain Division also hosts Mount Rainier Scenic Railroad.

In 1996 the City bought the Mountain Division from then-owner Weyerhaeuser, based largely on a daring business idea: would it be viable to convert the rail line into a "Train to the Mountain"—an exclusive railway that would whisk tourists from Tacoma to Mount Rainier National Park?

The largest volume of traffic on the Mountain Division began in June 2003 when Randles Sand & Gravel started loading crushed rock from their quarry at Eatonville, Washington, via conveyor (top picture) to air-dump gondola cars on the TRMW mainline (bottom picture). The product moved in unit train service via Tacoma Rail to Randles's wholesale operation in Frederickson, Washington. High operational costs resulted in negative margins and this once promising business came to an end in February 2006.

Tacoma Rail started operating the Mountain Division for the City's Public Works Division in November of 1998, but a formal agreement to do so wasn't adopted until 2004. The new division's stated mission: increase the vitality of the South Puget Sound area by significantly improving needed freight rail service and providing managed access to Mount Rainier National Park's two million annual visitors.

The entire Mountain Division covers 131 miles of track starting in Fife. It forks at Frederickson and travels separately to Chehalis and Morton. The

Rebuilding or replacement of several wooden timber trestles was required to restore rail service to the southwest Washington lumber manufacturing community of Morton located at the terminus of the Mountain Division's M-Line.

Morton route, used for the much-ballyhooed excursion train, badly needed an upgrade. Tacoma Rail was very successful in obtaining federal grants for upgrade of the basic rail infrastructure there.

The path itself had a long history. Developed originally as the Tacoma Eastern Railroad by brothers John F. and George E. Hart, the route began life in 1890 as a two-mile logging road at the head of Commencement Bay. The Hart brothers began to extend the railroad south toward the Mount Rainier foothills but went broke after a massive 1892 fire destroyed their Tacoma sawmill. The route lay fallow until the Yukon Gold Rush of 1899. With construction financing covertly provided by the Milwaukee (and labor provided mostly by Japanese immigrants, not the more prevalent Chinese, who were ostracized), the Tacoma Eastern passenger line ran regular passenger trains from both Seattle and Tacoma on tracks that passed through Eatonville and Elbe to Ashford, near the national park entrance, in late 1904 with the main freight line to Morton opening in 1910.

Prior to this, access to the mountain had only been by horseback. Tourism and timber became the line's primary businesses until the end of 1918, when the Tacoma Eastern Railroad's assets were consolidated, and its identity was absorbed by the Milwaukee Road. From that point until 1980, this mountain-ward branch of the Milwaukee was perennially among the most economically viable runs within the railroad's entire 11,000-mile network. In 1980, when the Milwaukee Road breathed its last in the Pacific Northwest, the former Tacoma Eastern portion of the railroad was sold to Weyerhaeuser Company, who used the line to move logs to the Port of Tacoma for international export.

TRAIN TO THE MOUNTAIN

From a commercial point of view, the passenger railroad connecting Tacoma with Mount Rainier National Park was intended to generate a complementary revenue source to the freight incomes earned by serving Frederickson clients. It would operate the passenger train at different times from the freight traffic, transporting visitors from Freighthouse Square along an increasingly scenic route toward the national park entrance. "The economic bubble was still building, and it had not burst," said Dennis Dean. "Spanaway Lumber was going to provide enough volume for that railroad to break even. We were running daily service. [Frederickson customer] Boeing was not every day, but because we had daily service up there for Spanaway Lumber and six to eight loads of lumber out of there a day, we picked up more customers."

When Tacoma Rail received the Mountain Division, U.S. Representative Norm Dicks (D-WA) became an enthusiastic supporter of excursion rail to Mount Rainier. *Public domain photo*

For its part, Spanaway agreed to ship at least 50 cars of finished lumber a month for the next two years, some $300,000 a year in revenue the railroad line expected to use to pay off its investment. Spanaway was betting on rail to boost efficiency and reduce the number of truck trips made each month by about two hundred. The company projected $350,000-a-year savings to invest $4 million in new plant capacity that could add sixty new workers.

On the excursion side, Paula Henry and others enthusiastically promoted the Train to the Mountain idea. When Tacoma Rail received the Mountain Division, Henry made the most of her relationships at the federal level, including that with U.S. Representative Norm Dicks, a veteran congressman who'd previously landed funds for Washington State interests as specific as

The GrandeLuxe leaving Tacoma for the TRMW in 2007. The GrandLuxe was a luxury train that was to have been a prototype for the "Train to the Mountain."

A July 30, 2007, test run of the Spirit of Washington Dinner Train, prior to its inaugural run on August 3.

A joint venture of Tacoma Rail and the Metropolitan Park District, the summertime, weekends-only "Train to Trek" ran from Freighthouse Square in Tacoma to Eatonville to visit the Northwest Trek Wildlife Park. The train made its final run in October 2009.

the Wine Grape Foundation Block ($325,000) and asparagus technology and production ($250,000). Representative Dicks became an enthusiastic supporter of excursion rail to Mount Rainier and made it his pet project. The result: Tacoma Rail received several grants from the Transportation Department.

Revenue from Frederickson freight traffic along the route was expected to offset any losses from the financially riskier tourist operation. However, despite several attempts over the following decade, no permanent tourist passenger railway was ever established on the line. The tourist railway never became viable. Both the American Orient Express and its owner GrandLuxe Rail Journeys used the line, but only occasionally, to carry passengers to the vicinity of the park as part of their rail programs touring the West. But GrandLuxe abruptly ceased operation in August 2008, when it was still providing passenger service to Mount Rainier.

The Spirit of Washington Dinner Train, running from Renton to Woodinville on the east side of Lake Washington, operated successfully for fifteen years. After expansion of Interstate 405 forced the closure of one of the rail bridges along its route, it relocated to Tacoma. Although the dinner train inaugurated its use of the Mountain Division's rails with great fanfare, the service was summarily discontinued after only three months leaving Tacoma Rail holding unpaid expenses of over $100,000.

A subsequent tourist train (also operating on city rails), the Great Northern Pacific, never actually launched its Rainier-bound service. About this same time, Train to Trek, a joint venture of Tacoma Rail and the Metropolitan Park District, also shuttered service after only three seasons, a victim of falling ridership. Tacoma Rail used its own passenger cars on this line, purchased from Amtrak. After two profitable seasons, the summertime, weekends-only train trip from Tacoma to Eatonville to visit the Northwest Trek Wildlife Park also failed financially, making its final run in October 2009.

With hindsight, it appears these various passenger plans—hearkening back to a time when a train outing was a special family event—were doomed by their own ambitious, but unrealistic, desire to tempt tourists off the highways and back onto the train. For although Mount Rainier was as popular as ever, modern tourists were motorized themselves.

POISON PILL

Business on the line never developed, despite $31 million in grant money. Ambitions for the line all but died by 2007, after a study showed track upgrades needed for the venture could cost as much as $24 million.

The $6.25 million debt incurred on the Mountain Division by covering operating losses with interfund loans from one city account to another comes due in 2017. Because of the way government accounting works with grant monies counted as revenue, it appeared from the financial statements that the Mountain Division was fine, despite the fact from a purely operational point of view it has lost money for many years. However, continuing interfund loans were established in an attempt to keep the cash balance positive. "The Train to the Mountain was about getting grant money when money was needed more in the Tidelands," said Dale King, current Tacoma Rail superintendent. "They were trying to develop new opportunities on all lines, rather than putting the money into places where the business already existed. We've shifted that now."

To alleviate some expense, Tacoma Rail has leased portions of the line to the Western Washington and Mount Rainier Scenic Railroads. The Western Washington Railroad operates on the southern end of the Chehalis line. The Mount Rainier Scenic Railroad has a depot in Elbe and a destination museum in Mineral from which they run a steam train seasonally.

"We started to recalibrate how and what we were submitting applications for," said Alan Matheson, current Tacoma Rail chief mechanical officer, who oversaw grant writing. "All of it was consistent with the vision, but it's just a different approach and sequencing. And then you get to a point where power shifts, other economic issues arise and so the doors slammed shut on federal [monies]." Tacoma Rail spent efficiently, but a seismic shift at the federal level meant grants dried up. While the flow of federal grant monies stopped, Tacoma Rail did successfully secure additional state grants for a time.

Selling the loss-generating road remains unlikely. Because of the money that is legally encumbered, the line has to be run by a government or quasi-government entity for 40 years. Tacoma Rail is only 10 years into the agreement, so unless it can find a governmental buyer, the Mountain Division remains a poison pill.

SIGNS OF SLOWDOWN

The slowing economy combined with the energy crisis in the Pacific Northwest resulted in slightly lower revenues in 2001. The closure of large, long-time customer Kaiser Aluminum alone accounted for a reduction of more than four thousand cars switched; the railroad did about a half million dollars less business ($8.2 million) in 2001 than in the previous year. In addition, the global slowdown affected container shipping and resulted in a 17 percent drop in switching activities.

One other notable activity during this timeframe: Tacoma Rail made its first-ever furloughs during the 2001 energy crisis. In mid-June that year, after 106 days off the job, the furloughed group of employees was given 30 days to report back. Ten of the 13 furloughed workers returned.

PIERCE COUNTY TERMINAL

In 2002, construction began on the Port of Tacoma's massive expansion centerpiece, the $210 million Pierce County Terminal. The largest such facility north of Los Angeles, Pierce County Terminal was designed to handle two of the world's biggest container ships at the same time, giving it the newfound ability to process a single ship docked at the terminal within 24 to 36 hours, a significant gain in turnaround efficiency. The new intermodal rail yard added twelve additional tracks to support it.

The 171-acre terminal on the Blair Waterway opened on January 28, 2005, with Marine Terminals Corporation managing operations. Taiwan-based Evergreen Marine, one of the world's largest shipping lines, holds a 20-year lease on the terminal and contributed $55 million for cranes and other equipment.

The new facility was served by five 1,600-ton cranes with an estimated annual capacity of 840,000 TEUs, or 20-foot-equivalent units, the industry measure of container volume. That one-third-volume increase in TEUs for Tacoma's port, coupled with the ability to now handle two ships simultaneously, led to a major, immediate uptick in business.

A fair statement to make during the intermodal era was, "As the Port goes, so goes Tacoma Rail." The year 2002 was one of the railroad's best years ever. Tacoma Rail saw operating revenues increase some 14.1 percent. Switching 70,401 cars that year— a record high number—Tacoma Rail ended 2002 with a net income of $1.2 million compared to a net loss of $9,000 just a year earlier.

The reason: the Port of Tacoma reported record shipping activity that same year. The rail system's quick response in alleviating a cargo backlog (following a 10-day, October longshoreman lockout) allowed the Port to stay up and running. The Tacoma Public Utilities annual report for that year states: "Tacoma Rail's immediate response and quick unloading time influenced shippers to unload in Tacoma instead of in other West Coast ports." Switching activities correspondingly rose by 17.6 percent.

Centerpiece of the Port of Tacoma, the $210 million Pierce County Terminal (PCT) launched in 2005. It has increased Tacoma's ability to handle the world's biggest container ships faster. The new intermodal terminal added eight miles of support tracks to the total track infrastructure. *Courtesy Port of Tacoma*

LOCOMOTIVE SERVICING AND THE DEAN BARN

Constructed in 2003 originally as an equipment storage building, the Dean Barn—the locomotive servicing facility named for past superintendent Dennis Dean—has become a hive of regular activity. If it weren't for the evolution of the Dean Barn into a functional locomotive-servicing area, Tacoma Rail would not have been able to provide the extraordinary value-added locomotive inspection and daily services it gives Tacoma Rail's Class I partners as part of its popular and financially successful locomotive service program.

Locomotive servicing there began in 2006 as a pilot project with the Union Pacific. Tracks into the area were upgraded and reconfigured to improve equipment movement flexibility inside the mechanical area in 2009, and additional features were added to enable the fueling, sanding, and light maintenance of locomotives in 2012.

The locomotive-servicing program has contributed to Tacoma Rail's competitiveness by way of helping to balance East/West locomotive power needs and further bolsters Tacoma Rail's "can do" approach toward customer service. In late 2006, Tacoma Rail put together a locomotive-servicing program to its two major carrier customers. The Union Pacific signed up, with the attraction of cutting an extra locomotive day of utilization by allowing the railroad to pick up fuel, service, and deliver power on-site in its Dean Barn facilities.

The servicing program was a big hit with the carriers, whose crews could now simply show up at the Tacoma Rail yard and depart with a fully prepared train. In 2007, Tacoma Rail serviced 1,069 locomotives. Following a 2011 facility upgrade to improve efficiencies, BNSF Railway signed on to the program in 2014. To date, the program has serviced more than 15,000 total locomotives.

Locomotive servicing brought the carriers substantial time and cost savings and more importantly provided value and deepened relationships between Tacoma Rail and the major railroads. Over time, saving thirty

to forty trains about four hours per start adds up. "The equation in railroading is that you have the cars, the locomotives and the people, and so right now we control cars and locomotives," said Dale King. "About half of the people are ours, and [for] the other half we rely on the Union Pacific and the BNSF Railway, who run the trains out of our terminal. So we are in much more control of our fate today."

EXCEPTIONAL TECHNOLOGY

Under the watchful eye of Dan McCabe, Tacoma Rail CIO/CFO, exceptional technology has become a hallmark of the modern era at Tacoma Rail. A confessed tech geek, McCabe oversees state-of-the-art monitoring, has pioneered concepts pertaining to "the paperless railroad," and even developed the software solution that is helping Tacoma Rail manage the rail yard—a need that developed, he says, for a simple but very good reason. "Before I arrived, Tacoma Rail was considered a black hole of information. Tacoma Rail knew where traffic was, but we didn't have a good means of communicating it. Mainlines and customers had a difficult time knowing where their traffic was. Now we're able to filter, sort, group, and format to create our own reports and data feeds to share information with our partners in multiple ways."

Using McCabe's digital program, Tacoma Rail can manage (and customers can view) trains, cars, and cargo and track footage online in near real time. "The customer is able to submit a switch request that prints out a custom sheet that goes out to our crews," said McCabe, whose creation attracted the attention of rail-related software makers. "In 2003, a major short line railroad software company was developing something similar. Their programmer said, 'We're actually going to have a web presence, you can utilize us.' And we said, 'No, we're good. We've already developed our own that fits our needs.'" Tacoma Rail is the only short line railroad in North America with this type of web presence. In the near future, McCabe hopes to incorporate geofencing (precise location data) and also remote-monitored locomotive telemetry.

With intermodal business at an all-time high, the Port of Tacoma experienced record activity in 2003, and Tacoma Rail turned in its new best year ever—increasing revenues by an astounding 18.8 percent. Tacoma Rail took in a net income of $1.3 million, with 85,017 cars switched.

Surging intermodal activity made the Port of Tacoma the statistical leader among seaports in the Pacific Northwest. The stronger than anticipated rebound of the national economy, combined with the port's extensive expansion, influenced carriers to diversify their port of entry from more congested areas of the country and to use Tacoma as a primary hub. The year also saw the launch of various local construction projects, including the relocation of the automobile import and processing center to the new Marshall Avenue auto facility. In addition, demurrage revenues (fees paid to Tacoma Rail due to undue detention of a railcar) increased $313,000 in 2003 to $766,000.

In this June 2012 image, new Tacoma Rail trucks are poised at TPU Fleet Management for delivery to the railroad to handle the newly acquired Grand Alliance intermodal business.

A commercial interchange train hauled by TMBL 1524 consisting of covered hopper cars and tank cars approaches Bullfrog Junction. A critical piece of infrastructure, Bullfrog Junction is where Tacoma Rail connects with the North American rail network via BNSF Railway and the Union Pacific Railroad.

THE CAPITAL DIVISION

With the formal addition of the Capital Division to its operations in late 2004—established through the lease of two BNSF Railway branch lines and the purchase of the freight franchise on another—Tacoma Rail began to experience a period of "expense creep" associated with the expansion of its geographical reach. "At the time, the economy was still building," said Dennis Dean. "Industry needed rail and this was a good deal at the time and allowed BNSF Railway to cut its losses. Economically, it made sense."

Financially speaking, the three disconnected branch lines known as the Capital Division contributed right away. Switching achieved an all-time high with 97,417 cars, shattering the 2003 previous best by more than 10,000 cars. The railroad generated a dramatic increase in switching revenues, from both the intermodal and the auto import traffic.

Rates remained the same for a few years, offset by the increase in volumes. Because rate increases stayed under the actual rate of inflation, this translated to more profit for the mainlines, or technically cheaper rates to customers. With the Port of Tacoma's expansion and a corresponding increase in the number of carriers now using it as a primary hub, the port continued to report record-breaking shipping activity.

The Tacoma Command Center opened in May 2005, with an oversight committee consisting of representatives from the Port of Tacoma, BNSF Railway, Union Pacific, and then-Tacoma Rail Assistant Superintendent Paula Henry. The idea was for all three railroads and port terminals to be able to communicate more effectively by meeting regularly to coordinate their activities. While money and time constraints prevented the full physical facility from launching, the venture ultimately morphed into an online virtual center still in use today, named the BEX (Business Exchange). The BEX is hosted and maintained by the BNSF Railway and is offered at some other ports and inland terminals; however, it was initially developed for Tacoma Rail and the Port traffic to improve railcar velocity through the railroad's Bullfrog Junction entry point.

DEAN RIDES OFF

On December 24, 2005, Dennis Dean called it a career. "I'm not retiring, I'm switching to seven-day weekends," said the 45-year railroad man. When he left, switching activities were at an all-time high with back-to-back record years: 97,417 cars switched in 2004 and 118,474 switched in 2005. The dramatic increase came as the Port of Tacoma was also experiencing record-breaking intermodal and automobile traffic.

Dean's era saw the expansion from three train crews (and forty employees) working five 16-hour days to 18 locomotives (and 105 employees) running a continuous 24-hour operation. His tenure coincided with an interesting moment in American railroading. Congress effectively deregulated freight rail transportation during the 1980s, eliminating many Class I carriers but ushering in more than three hundred short line railroads—all of which needed secure, reliable service.

Dean put together the combined operations in the port and the acceptance of the Mountain Division, somewhat reluctantly, under an operating agreement where ownership stayed with the City, but Tacoma Rail ran the operation. At the end of his career, Tacoma Rail acquired the Capital Division.

Under his watch, Tacoma Municipal Belt Line expanded from a small, port-based terminal switching company into a Class III short line railroad. Tacoma Municipal Belt Line grew from about 30 miles of track in the port into Tacoma Rail with its present-day 204 miles of operating territory.

Dennis Dean's "ask for forgiveness, not permission" philosophy served him well over his career. At times, it may have alienated him from some, but by working outside of the system, Dean established the solid foundation that remains beneath Tacoma Rail to this day.

PAULA HENRY STEPS UP

Dean's successor, Paula Henry, brought a diplomatic savvy to Tacoma Rail that her predecessors couldn't. Well known in the public utility and city government, Henry came to Tacoma Municipal Belt Line in 1998 when its revenue and operating costs were much smaller compared to today's and at a time when the company's budgeting process was messy and its financial results were gloomy. Immediately she became involved in the expansion phase of the latter part of the Dennis Dean era, cultivating relationships that would secure funding for the company. Although the Henry era began on a high note because of her fresh energy and ideas, volatility marked the next two years.

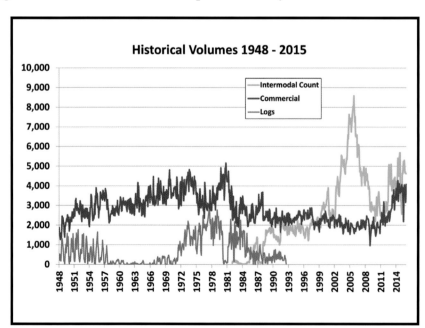

Studying the General Code of Operating Rules (GCOR) in the Mobile Training Facility classroom are (left to right): conductor Keith Shaw, road foreman of engines Marc Robertson, locomotive engineer Andrew Rose, and conductor Andrew Ison.

Tacoma Rail road foreman of engines Marc Robertson brings a train out of the gulch through Freighthouse Square on the New York Airbrake Simulator (NYAB) located in the Mobile Training Facility.

Acquired in 2011, TMBL 2100 is the only GenSet engine Tacoma Rail has and is the first all-new locomotive Tacoma Rail has ever purchased. It is powered by three separate 700-horsepower diesel engines that power up as needed. *Photo by Steve Carter*

RECESSION AND RESILIENCE

CHAPTER SEVEN

Despite exponential growth of 75 percent from 2000 to 2005, the mid-2000s proved to be a challenging time for Tacoma Rail. The earmarks era in Congress brought a sudden deluge of governmental monies, but the spigot would soon be shut off.

As fuel costs rose, intermodal volumes dropped as carriers optimized well usage on doublestack trains, testing the limits of infrastructure. Tacoma's ambition, to compete against both Los Angeles/Long Beach and Seattle as a West Coast port of choice, brought rapid desire for expansion.

The year 2006 for Tacoma Rail also marked the start of a seven-year period without a single hire in the operating crafts (switch operator, now called conductor). But there was hiring in the other parts of the business during that time, mostly to address vacancies resulting from attrition. Although the Port of Tacoma reported an increase of containers handled that year, 2006 saw a dramatic drop in intermodal railcar traffic. And when fuel prices changed faster than its tariff rate process could handle, Tacoma Rail recognized the need for a fuel surcharge.

Nevertheless, the Port saw increasing volumes, yet rail wasn't the cause. The reason: more articulations per railcar (i.e. more five wells vs. single wells) and a mainline well utilization initiative rewarded logistical planning and penalized shippers for not loading intermodal cars efficiently. Simple economics: cram more freight on a more aerodynamic single train and haul in a fuel-efficient manner, mainline revenue generation per container well would increase.

During the economic slowdown of 2006, Tacoma Rail again relied on furloughing workers to try to temporarily cut costs but preserve jobs. During the timeframe, Superintendent Paula Henry issued seven furloughs for a period of about six months each. Three of the seven returned.

TMBL 2100, rebuilt from a GP40 chassis by National Railway Equipment Company (NRE), stands poised with a commercial cut of railcars. Designated a 3GS21B-DE by NRE, it is powered by three, 700-horsepower, Cummins diesel engines (gensets) that come on line randomly as the throttle position increases. Theoretically this technology was designed to reduce emissions while optimizing the locomotive's tractive effort.

By all accounts, Henry had a gift for working the dynamics of government to acquire resources Tacoma Rail desperately needed. Her focus was on the longer-term development of the company, rather than on the basic short-term infrastructural upgrades needed to pull the railroad even with existing high volumes.

After the success of Pierce County Terminal, Port officials wanted to tighten their grip on handling container growth and press the growing advantage Tacoma was enjoying as an intermodal-shipping alternative to the port of Los Angeles/Long Beach. In 2007, the Port launched a project to build another state-of-the-art intermodal terminal, this one to host Nippon Yusen Kaisha Line (NYK) on the Blair Peninsula. Acquiring Tideflats acreage through both purchase and eminent domain, the Port required two existing Tacoma Rail commercial customers to relocate. One of them, Harris Rebar, opted to move its operations to Frederickson.

When the Great Recession occurred, the Blair project was mothballed and the newly cleared Tideflats land lay fallow. In 2010, citing declining cargo volumes and cost increases in the development plan, the Port of Tacoma decided to shelve the planned $300 million, 168-acre terminal on the Blair Waterway for NYK, which would have started calling in 2012. Costs were badly underestimated, with the projected $800 million project expense quickly rising to $1.2 billion before the whole thing was called off. Nippon Yusen Kaisha came to the port anyway, sharing space with Horizon Line at an existing terminal.

Leaders of the Port, including Executive Director Tim Farrell, blamed the global recession for the failure of the 2007 Blair NYK terminal project. The Port wound up spending $190 million in the deal, $146 million alone on real estate. Farrell was dismissed afterwards.

MOUNTAIN DIVISION TROUBLES

By 2007, the Mountain Division included 131 miles of track with 23 sidings. With its two branch lines, Chehalis and Morton (which included the Train to the Mountain), the division grew from three customers in its inaugural year to 13 customers in just eight years. From 1998 to 2007, the division had generated $10 million in revenue and had secured an astounding $21.9 million in grants.

But according to past superintendent Dennis Dean, given the condition of the track, particularly on the Morton side, another decade or so of upgrades was required. Although volume projections were optimistic, reality intervened. The previous partnership with the City, variability in the rail volumes and revenue generation, grants, and the increasing accumulation of debt were all factors that would surely continue to affect the rail line's competitiveness. And the Great Recession had yet to come.

A 2008 study by consultants HDR found the Mountain Division couldn't be maintained under its current scenario. The report proclaimed that only by keeping the first 14 miles (Tacoma to Frederickson) could the rail line be sustained. With freight revenue concentrated at Frederickson, and existing traffic volumes insufficient to cover costs, the study went on to recommend overall rates be increased and ownership transferred to Tacoma Public Utilities. Tacoma Public Utilities wouldn't take it on because of the associated debt and grant obligations that would come with the transfer.

The MacMillan Piper transload facility (railcars to containers) in Frederickson began in 2006 and ended in 2010. Pacific Steel and Recycling now operates in the location. One of Tacoma Rail's larger commercial customers, Mac-Pip operates two facilities in the Tideflats.

HENRY DEPARTS

On March 31, 2008, Paula Henry resigned her post as superintendent of Tacoma Rail, leaving for a private rail industry job. During her time with Tacoma Rail, she was instrumental in hiring several key executives who are still in management today, including Terminal Superintendent Tim Flood (who joined in 2006), a former BNSF Railway employee who was at the time rail superintendent for Marine Terminals Corporation at Pierce County Terminal; Chief Mechanical Officer Alan Matheson (2005); CIO and CFO Daniel McCabe (2002), who was initially hired via contract while completing college; and Assistant Superintendent of Administration Lori Daniels (1999). Paula Henry always believed in her employees and was often heard to say, "I'd put my team up against anybody, in any other railroad, or for that matter, a lot of different industries."

While Dennis Dean gets much of the credit for the era of Belt Line expansion, Paula Henry was highly involved as well. However, her style and background were different; rather than sinking into the minutiae of railroading, she focused her energies on building strategically vital political relationships, many of which ultimately benefited Tacoma Rail. Despite the turbulence created by port drama, furloughs, and Mountain Division woes during her 28-month term, she left behind a talented team and a focus on development and process that endures today.

HARDY RESTORES STABILITY

When Henry departed, Tacoma Public Utilities Director Bill Gaines asked Alan Hardy, the rail line's 53-year-old assistant superintendent, to assume the role of interim superintendent. Hardy had joined Tacoma Rail in 2004 as roadmaster, hired by Dean to restore standards, refocus the railroad on regulatory issues, and analyze and upgrade track structure. Instantly Hardy restored a sense of clarity in the organization that had been missing for some time.

Hardy also brought his concern for regulatory compliance and safety to his new post and was willing to spend the money necessary to ensure safe operations. An old school railroader, he had spent nearly 30 years working rail in Florida and all over the western United States before landing a job at Tacoma Rail. He promoted Tim Flood to manager of operations. Tenacious and energetic, Flood had a lot of Class I experience and effected a turnaround in that area.

Hardy served well in the interim position for eight months before Dale King was named the new Tacoma Rail superintendent. Still with Tacoma Rail today, Hardy's focus remains on operating a safe and environmentally sound railroad. He works with the Federal Railroad Administration (FRA), attends Short Line Association meetings, and interprets regulations to keep Tacoma Rail on the cutting edge of the industry.

MR. KING

In a span of 10 months in 2008, Tacoma Rail had three superintendents. Change always creates uncertainty. However, counterintuitive though it may sound, it was during this timeframe that King lay the groundwork for a surge in momentum still felt today in the organization.

Dale King had grown up in New Jersey and was a lifelong railroader with a corporate background. He got his start in rail at age 19 as a signalman and drawbridge captain for the Central Railroad Company of New Jersey. He later worked for Conrail, the Burlington Northern, and Willamette Industries in railroad and transportation management and sales before landing with Weyerhaeuser. There, King was appointed director of rail services, overseeing the company's five short line railroad operations. In December 2008 he joined Tacoma Rail.

As extensive as his background and experience was, Dale King could not have picked a worse time to join the company. The Great Recession hit in September and was in full force by December when the U.S. gross domestic product (GDP) plummeted. King arrived on the scene just as the nation's headlines were announcing a grim economic downturn was underway. The effects were felt across the nation, and locally a sharp, 25 percent decline was reported in port-related railcar volume—the engine of the rail business in Tacoma.

Dale King, concerned here about rising floodwaters, was as equally focused on the rising tide of red ink during the first two years of his tenure as Tacoma Rail superintendent.

THE GREAT RECESSION AND RECOVERY

The year 2009 saw 60-year lows in commercial traffic and the departure of Maersk Shipping to Seattle, causing a 30 percent decline in Tacoma Rail revenue and two years of million-dollar losses.

King did not sit idly by. To address the problem of declining revenues, he and Tacoma Rail reduced the rate on loaded intermodal platforms and established an empty intermodal platform charge. The idea was to provide incentive to the shipping lines to balance their traffic flows while Tacoma Rail received compensation for all intermodal activity. Commercial rates were kept the same to help customers keep freight moving at the continued low price while recovering from the worst of the recession. Although the entire plan took two years to wind its way through the political process, in the end it proved to be the railroad's turning point out of the Great Recession.

POTHOLE POLITICS

The latest movement toward ditching the municipal railroad came in 2009 during the recession. City infrastructure was falling apart, symbolized by an abundance of potholes in area roads. That June, an opinion article in the *Tacoma News Tribune* suggested the City should sell the railroad and use the proceeds to repair potholes. Its logic: since few cities own railroads, neither should Tacoma. Lacking a profit motive, the article theorized, the publicly owned municipal line didn't lay off people as efficiently as one that was privately held would have.

The piece included comments from Pacific Harbor Line Inc., which at the time had expressed interest in buying Tacoma Rail. Sell the railroad to them, concluded the author—but before you do, open up the sale to competitive bidding. Sell and use the one-time windfall to resurface city streets. And start the time-consuming process of city council approval and ballot vote now.

Tacoma Public Utilities Director Bill Gaines soon responded with a *News Tribune* op-ed of his own. In his reply, Gaines explained private ownership and inevitable substantial rate hikes would damage the Port of Tacoma's competitiveness, in turn potentially harming employment and the local economy. Gaines defended the railroad's economic situation, stating that to avoid layoffs, Tacoma Rail hadn't filled vacant jobs, had placed restrictions on overtime pay, and had reduced crews and scheduled runs. The timing of a hypothetical sale was poor, Gaines wrote, stating that placing a value on the enterprise in a downturn, with lower volumes at the port, would be bad business. Such a decision, he wrote, "should be undertaken through a deliberative process . . . not as a reaction to overtures from private operators [seeking] to further their own financial objectives."

The entire episode played out on the op-ed pages, but stirred the time-honored question, "Why *does* Tacoma own a railroad?" History is one reason; difficulty could be another. Any sale would have to go out for public bid. The City and the highest bidder would then put the sale of a public utility on the table for the citizens of Tacoma to vote on. "The railroad had been up for sale a number of times," said Dennis Dean recently. "If you ask me, selling it would've been shortsighted. It would have been a one-shot revenue deal for the City, with no future revenue for Tacoma."

Empty intermodal well-cars are being repositioned into deep storage southward from downtown Centralia to Chehalis on the Mountain Division C-Line in July 2012. The move was made with Chehalis-Centralia Railroad's 1916 Baldwin-built 2-8-2 steam locomotive No. 15 due to the 17 miles of stored railcars blocking Tacoma Rail locomotive access from the north.

A STORAGE "STILL LIFE"

The dismal economic climate offered the opportunity to stop the bleeding on the Mountain Division by filling it with storage cars idled by the recession. Taking immediate action to monetize the miles of little-used track in rural Pierce, Thurston, and Lewis Counties, King offered four major railcar leasing companies storage of their idle container cars—cars that had been sidelined by low import activities.

Tacoma Rail contracted with all four to "park" their railroad cars on Mountain Division tracks near Fort Lewis and on the west side of Interstate 5, near Centralia. At its peak, the still-life procession of cars reached nearly seventeen miles in length. The car leasing companies typically paid Tacoma Rail about $1.50 per day per platform in storage fees. With hundreds of cars in storage, those storage fees brought in six-figure annual revenues the Mountain Division had never before been in a position to generate.

King also moved to defray track maintenance costs—a perennial financial sore spot for the Mountain Division. The railroad offered to lease portions of rail line to others with the stipulation they would maintain the tracks used.

THE "DALE FURLOUGHS"

The 2009 volume drop was not a standard railroad-industry cyclical ebb and flow. All the customers were pulling back. Tacoma Rail's net income, having achieved a 2007 record level of $2.4 million (on 83,416 cars switched), drove off a cliff to an overall net loss of $9,170 on 60,924 cars switched.

King, who had just been through layoffs at Weyerhaeuser, sought another way to get through the downturn without having to terminate positions. All through 2009, he kept everyone's job intact. "When you look out and all you see is bare tracks in the yard, this doesn't portend very well," said Tim Flood. "We were very cost-conscious. We held on. Dale didn't furlough when maybe we should have."

As of the 2010 census, Tacoma had a population of 198,397, an increase of 2.5 percent over the previous decade. Perhaps the biggest news of the year for Tacoma Rail were the cancellations of the Blair project by the Port of Tacoma and the Train to the Mountain by the City. Inside the railroad, however, the chief concern was whether people would still have jobs.

In January 2010 King announced furloughs for seven switchmen who were to be brought back in, two days per month, to undergo training and to perform fill-in duties while regular employees attended training sessions. With the required monthly minimal time on site, the furloughed employees were able to maintain their medical benefits and credited service toward their railroad retirement pensions. "We based it on the cost that we'd incur to retrain folks, what we've already invested in these employees, and it's kind of the least we could do," said Lori Daniels, assistant superintendent of administration. "If we don't do these things, bring them back two days a month—one for recurring training, the second day they would go out and work while we brought other employees in to train."

King's furlough idea kept trained staffers coming in. Two of the furloughed employees took advantage of the opportunity to train in another craft during the furlough status. The seven were able to maintain their creditable service for retirement, retain healthcare benefits, and get a little bit of pay. At the same time, Tacoma Rail could potentially get them back.

Tacoma Rail had furloughed 13 people in 2001, retaining 10 of them after nearly four months away. During the furlough of 2006, lasting six months, seven employees were affected and three came back. In the old-school Tacoma Rail fashion, the situation would have been handled differently. The "Dale Furloughs," as they became known, were another story. More than seven months later, all seven employees returned.

STYLE

Under King, and Hardy before him, there are higher performance standards, more process checks and—beginning with Dean and extended to Henry's grants—infrastructure has improved.

King operates Tacoma Rail following a five-point credo staff has actually inscribed on lobby walls:

- Live Safety
- Take Care of the Customer
- Work Hard
- Have Fun
- Respect One Another

The job seems tailor-made for King, who puts in long hours and makes decisions from a professional "default mode" that can best be summed up by a single term: compassion. "I have the best job in the greatest industry," King has said.

"By taking it from a reactive to an anticipatory approach over time, Dale has instilled a sense of pride that really wasn't here," said Alan Matheson. "You now have increasingly stronger and more reliable infrastructure and equipment, and people that are now proud to be Tacoma Rail. Things are trending in a more positive, more productive direction."

TACOMA RAIL LOCOMOTIVE FLEET OVERVIEW

Tacoma Rail's current approach to locomotive power is as forward thinking as it has ever been. After nine decades of making do with pre-owned, "old warhorse" locomotives using yesterday's technology, Tacoma Rail has reinvigorated its fleet.

In 2013 the line made a diesel purchase of its own, with high-powered, state-of-the-art locomotives that are Tier 3 emission compliant. Tacoma Rail is financing on a five-year, lease-to-own arrangement. At the conclusion of this first all-new purchase, says King, "We will have repowered six out of the 14 engines that we originally had when I came on, so almost half of our fleet will be year 2011 or newer locomotives."

Tacoma Rail will have cut the average age of its fleet by about two-thirds. In the meantime, the railway is servicing Union Pacific road locomotives. After several years of asking, Tacoma Rail got the contract to service BNSF Railway locomotives as well.

Loco #	Purchased	Builder	Model	HP	Engine Type	Weight in Pounds	Year Built
3000	5/26/1999	EMD	SD-40	3,000	645E3	368,000	1968
3001	6/11/2001	EMD	SD-40-2	3,000	645E3	368,000	1985
1521	5/3/2003	EMD	MP-1500	1,500	645E	248,000	1982
1522	5/3/2003	EMD	MP-1500	1,500	645E	248,000	1982
1523	5/3/2003	EMD	MP-1500	1,500	645E	248,000	1982
1524	5/3/2003	EMD	MP-1500	1,500	645E	248,000	1982
3801	5/3/2005	EMD	GP 38-2	2,000	645E	250,000	1979
3802	5/3/2005	EMD	GP 38-2	2,000	645E	250,000	1979
4001	9/30/2005	EMD	GP-40-M	2,300	645E3	245,000	1965
4002	12/30/2005	EMD	GP-40-M	2,300	645E3	245,000	1965
2100	8/26/2011	NRE	3GS21B-DE	2,100	(3) QSK-19	268,000	2011
2200	11/21/2011	EMD	GP-22eco	2,000	8-710-ECO	245,000	2011
2201	12/1/2011	EMD	GP-22eco	2,000	8-710-ECO	245,000	2011
7001	Leased 11/1/2014	EMD	SD70 Ace-P4	4,300	710G3C-ES 16	408,000	2013
7002	Leased 11/1/2015	EMD	SD70 Ace-P4	4,300	710G3C-ES 16	408,000	2013

The SD70s, with a little help from the smaller GenSet 2100, escort another train to Frederickson. *Photo by Steve Carter*

A look at the first Grand Alliance train as it leaves the Port of Tacoma's Washington United Terminal on July 3, 2012.

This 2012 image of Tacoma Rail's main yard illustrates traffic diversification, key to addressing business volume fluctuations in each commodity segment. A crude oil unit train is flanked by an empty intermodal unit train (called a baretable) and other traffic moving in plain boxcars, covered hopper cars, and refrigerated boxcars.

RECOVERY AND ALL-NEW POWER

The first layoffs in eight years and the suspension of major capital projects helped stabilize Tacoma Rail's financial situation, setting the stage for slow recovery in 2011. Tacoma Rail saw a 30 percent overall drop in traffic volume during the recession, 20 percent on commercial traffic, and 40 percent on intermodal business. The intermodal loaded-to-empty platform ratio dropped from 90 percent to 60 percent. Since the pricing structure in place at the time allowed no compensation for the movement of empty platforms, Tacoma Rail suffered a $2 million operating loss in the 2009–2010 biennium.

The City of Tacoma and Tacoma Rail entered into a new, five-year operating agreement for the Mountain Division in 2011, with the objective of retiring debt and transferring divisional ownership from the City to Tacoma Rail. Around this same time, Tacoma Rail began making a conscious effort to modernize the locomotive fleet, retiring or replacing older power and focusing on environmental stewardship and the installation of more modern technology such as idle reduction features.

The beginning of Environmental Protection Agency grants to repower three locomotives made it possible for Tacoma Rail to obtain an essentially new locomotive. (Tacoma Rail provided a locomotive core/shell which was stripped down and refurbished.) In 2011 the Environmental Protection Agency put out a call for bids through their Diesel Emission Reduction Act (DERA) projects. The grant had a deadline tied to it having to do with shovel-ready projects and pumping money back into the economy. Tacoma Rail's submission scored second to winner BNSF Railway, who later elected to pass. "All the sudden here came [Washington State] Department of Ecology saying, 'We're happy to give this to you, but just know that it's a hard deadline,'" said Matheson.

As part of the Energy Policy Act of 2005 and the American Recovery and Reinvestment Act of 2009, the Environmental Protection Agency was offering locomotive repower grants through its National Clean Diesel Campaign in order to replace inefficient diesel locomotives with new Tier 2 units that were compliant with Tier 2 emission standards. Having been awarded this grant to repower three locomotives in a three-year period, BNSF Railway elected to pass through its rights. Environmental Protection Agency informed Tacoma Rail, which originally proposed matching funds, that it had been second in line in the repower proposal and invited Tacoma Rail to participate—with the caveat it would have just one year to complete the repower.

Tacoma Rail received a Tier 3 compliant GenSet locomotive in August 2011, just in time for its annual open house. TMBL 2100 is the only GenSet engine Tacoma Rail has and is powered by three separate 700-horsepower diesel engines that power up as needed.

THE GRAND ALLIANCE

The year 2012 brought some of the best news in years to Tacoma Rail. In March, the Grand Alliance (GA) of shipping lines announced it would relocate from Seattle to Tacoma in July.

The coming addition of three substantial NYK line, Hapag-Lloyd, and Orient Overseas Container Line (OOCL) arrivals each week at the Port—with containers carrying auto parts, electronics, and other consumer goods from the Pacific Rim—meant an immediate, dramatic increase in shipping volumes for the Port of Tacoma's Washington United Terminal.

The genesis of the shift began in 2009, when NYK announced its intention not to renew a Seattle lease when it was set to expire in 2012. Soon after the new year, the two other lines followed suit, and by July 1 they had joined NYK in the move to the Washington United Terminal in Tacoma. To say the arrival of the Grand Alliance consortium to Tacoma was "met with open arms" would be an understatement. Ecstatic was more like it.

Tacoma Rail began a crash program to prepare for the new volume. Overnight, longshore, trucking, and rail hiring began. Service started on July 3 and in that month alone, Tacoma Rail's intermodal business rose more than 40 percent. From the 2008 financial meltdown, Tacoma's port economy had suffered along with other industries with international intermodal shipping falling by some 40 percent. Where container volumes had bottomed out after the Maersk Line left Tacoma in 2010 and moved to Seattle, now cargo would be unloaded and loaded at each of the five major ship terminals at the Port of Tacoma. For Tacoma Rail, this meant moving the majority of those containers from the docks to the mainline railroads for transcontinental distribution.

After six years without adding a single switchman (or switch supervisor), Tacoma Rail hired nine new employees. It also replaced three aging locomotives dating to mid-2011 with powerful, emission-efficient units, and it moved forward with plans to upgrade rail yard infrastructure and dock routes.

An eco-friendly pair works the newly rebuilt U.S. Oil facility, 2015. *Photo by Steve Carter*

Also in 2012, U.S. Oil & Refining Company announced a switch from Alaskan crude oil to oil pumped from the Bakken oil fields in North Dakota. Bakken is the largest oil drilling region outside of Texas and the third biggest in the country, producing more than 1.2 million barrels a day. This decision meant instead of shipping on ocean-going tankers, delivery would be effected by rail-based tank cars beginning in October—a shift whose impact would be a huge boost to Tacoma Rail's volume. The result was the first $2 million revenue month in the history of the company.

Serving automotive, aviation, and marine industry fuel needs, U.S. Oil announced it would bring even more train cars to Tacoma Rail and pledged to give the railroad $1 million to build three new tracks to accommodate traffic. They also began immediately building a crude oil unit train unloading facility.

Combined with the arrival of the Grand Alliance, the U.S. Oil unit trains raised Tacoma Rail traffic volume by 50 percent virtually overnight. Tacoma Rail's neighbor in the Tideflats since 1950, U.S. Oil promised funds that account for about 75 percent of the overall track-addition project cost. Two of the new tracks will enable the railroad to approach U.S. Oil's facility from two sides, and the third will store cars from U.S. Oil's non-unit train business (one hundred cars or less). Once the new tracks are complete, the railroad can process up to 106 railcars a day—a 30 percent increase from the current amount.

On the whole, the mid-2000s were a heady time of both bold expansion—a revenue-rich period during which the railroad seemed ready to really take off—and of sputtering regression brought on by larger economic weakness. There was debt, but there was also modernization. Perhaps Tacoma Rail's innovative use of 17 miles of its track to temporarily store cargo-less railcars serves as the signature metaphor that best illustrated this era of progress, pullback, and then uncertainty—followed by a concerted, strategic resumption of activity.

U.S. Oil & Refining's 2012 decision to switch from Alaska (ocean tanker) to Bakken (tank car) crude oil resulted in the first $2 million revenue month in the history of Tacoma Rail. Bakken is the largest oil drilling region outside of Texas and the third biggest in the country, producing more than 1.2 million barrels a day. *Photo by Mick Klass*

Angled view, "Before." The refurb project of TMBL 201 was also an opportunity to get useful work out of injured employees who could no longer serve as switchmen—two were carpenters, two were handymen, and one was a professional painter. After two years of work they produced the Mobile Training Facility (MTF), whose conversion cost came in about $10,000 less than the usual single-wide trailer office purchase.

The Mobile Training Facility began as a 1967 Union Pacific steel caboose, UP 025643, which Tacoma Rail had acquired in 1990. It eventually became unsafe to use and was replaced. Below left is an interior shot of the TMBL 201 as it undergoes its transformation. Below right shows the facility just prior to its completion as the office of the road foreman of engines.

Angled view, "After." Starting in 2011, Tacoma Rail refurbished the caboose, which now serves as the Mobile Training Facility, equipped with meeting space and a New York Air Brake locomotive training simulator.

The Tacoma Rail Safety Committee regularly met in the Mobile Training Facility prior to the installation of the locomotive simulator in 2013. The Safety Committee members, front row left to right, are Tim Flood, Lori Luscher, Joshua Banks, Clayton Hoffman III. Back row are the late Mike Lynch, Andy Miller, Phil Schwiesow, Marc Robertson, Gary Anten, and Dale King.

TACOMA PUBLIC UTILITIES

The first trip on the
Capital Division in
2004, crossing the
Nisqually River on
the BNSF mainline.

TRAIN KEPT A ROLLIN'

CHAPTER EIGHT

Challenged from its earliest days by persistent debt, plagued by subpar infrastructure during the last half-century, and often caught in political headwinds regarding its very existence, Tacoma Rail has come a long way in the last one hundred years.

Day and night, Tacoma Rail's distinctive red and white locomotives haul goods across the marshy Tideflats of Tacoma's northwest side (an area of inlets and estuaries near the mouth of the Puyallup River) out of the Port of Olympia in Tacoma Rail's Capital Division and south to industrial customers near Frederickson on the City of Tacoma-owned Mountain Division.

Current Superintendent and Chief Operating Officer Dale King reports to Tacoma Public Utilities Director William Gaines. King is surrounded by a talented and experienced managerial team, many of whom began working for Tacoma Rail during the era of Paula Henry, King's predecessor. A quick look at Tacoma Rail's overall ecosystem shows Tacoma Public Utilities' overseers, the Tacoma Public Utilities Board and the Tacoma City Council. With frequent inspections, the Federal Railroad Administration (FRA) oversees Tacoma Rail safety matters, the Surface Transportation Board regulates rates, and the Washington Utilities and Transportation Commission enforces safety standards and regulations.

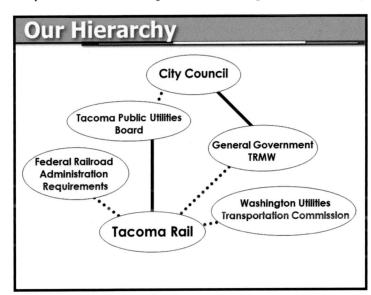

Our Hierarchy

- City Council
- Tacoma Public Utilities Board
- General Government TRMW
- Federal Railroad Administration Requirements
- Washington Utilities Transportation Commission
- Tacoma Rail

WORKING ON THE RAILROAD

In 2015 the workforce at Tacoma Rail is budgeted to reach 121 employees, up from a low of 89 during the Great Recession. "Tacoma Rail has one of the highest paid railroad workforces in the country," said Dennis Dean. "You can go to a lot of railroads where the union wages are significantly less. We have work rules that are more flexible, and we have employees who are at the top of their ability to serve the customer. That rubs off."

Conductor John Say, Tacoma Rail's most senior employee, enjoys the independent challenge. "Every day we go out, we get our paperwork and tools that we need, and then we try to do the work in an efficient manner, with the least amount of moves," said Say. "It could be a 90-degree scorcher outside, or if it's 20 degrees and there's snow all over, we still have to go out and do the work, and we get by with those challenges. It's self-rewarding, knowing that I can go out and do a good job and things get done and we get our customers taken care of."

"This is a new era for Tacoma Rail with better standards, more checks and improved infrastructure," said conductor Clayton Hoffman. "While the rules will provide you a safe work environment to an extent, there's another level of being able to trust the person you work with. Truly, it's a brotherhood out here."

FULL STEAM AHEAD

Since 1995, Tacoma Rail has experienced exponential growth, rising to its current levels of 250,000 revenue moves per year and attaining an enviable 96 percent on-time service performance. Switching activities increased in 2014 by 8,771 cars (8.8 percent) to 108,137, up from 99,366 in 2013. Operating results for Tacoma Rail in 2014 indicated a slight decrease in intermodal traffic—owing to labor negotiations between the Pacific Maritime Association (PMA) and the International Longshore and Warehouse Union (ILWU), which slowed container traffic flow—and an increase in non-intermodal traffic.

Tacoma Rail is on the verge of transforming from a big Class III into a Class II short line railroad. The railroad acquired all its inland territory during roughly this same timeframe and Tacoma Rail went from being a belt line located solely in the Tideflats to adding the Mountain Division (1998) and then the Capital Division (2004)—a considerable geographic spread compared to its first 85 years of existence.

A Tacoma Rail locomotive rolls across Capital Lake en route to Belmore.

Percival Creek flooding on the Belmore Line washed out a 100-foot section of roadbed following winter storms in 2007.

The first expansion took place with the Mountain Division (call sign TRMW), consisting of the old Tacoma Eastern Railroad, which established its first line south of Tacoma in 1887 (to reach forest areas around Mount Rainier) and later extended the line up to Morton. In Frederickson, the Tacoma Eastern split to Chehalis, Washington.

Today serving about 20 customers, the Capital Division consists of three different lines:

- The Belmore Line runs from East Olympia, where it connects to the BNSF Railway's main line, to Belmore southwest of Olympia, where an industrial park is served. Of note, the track from East Olympia to downtown Olympia is the former Union Pacific Olympia Line and is still owned by the Union Pacific. The BNSF leased from Union Pacific it when their track to Olympia was abandoned for an extension of Interstate 5 and subsequently included those running rights in its lease to Tacoma Rail.

- The Quadlok Line runs from St. Clair, south of Nisqually Junction on the main line of the BNSF Railway three miles to Quadlok, to serve customer International Paper.

- The Lakeview Line runs north from Nisqually Junction to South Tacoma, part of the former Northern Pacific Prairie Line.

Diversification has also helped position Tacoma Rail for continued success. Where the sources of business in 2008 were divided about 80 percent intermodal and 20 percent commercial, today it's a 50-50 split, making the company less vulnerable to the ups and downs of any given industry.

Cost-saving measures and the increase in railcar storage services during the down economy helped raise the net income of the Mountain Division in 2012. Washouts are one more thing the company overcomes; although the Morton side of the Mountain Division line continued to have difficulties due to washouts, leases were forged on both sides of the fork to reduce maintenance costs.

The year 2013 began a string of record revenue months that continued for two years until labor strife at West Coast ports arrested the run. A new 20-year operating agreement was established between the Port of Tacoma and Tacoma Rail giving the rail line unprecedented control of its future as the sole provider of rail service to the Port.

Sale of the "Freighthouse Square-to-TR Junction" portion of the Mountain Division to Sound Transit was concluded in early 2015. An interlocal agreement with Lewis County and the City of Chehalis, if fully implemented, will see the south 20 miles of the line (paralleling Interstate 5) divested by the end of 2016 to those entities.

A key revenue driver for Tacoma Rail has been the rise of intermodal transportation, which connected the municipal line to the larger global economy and helped establish and differentiate the Port of Tacoma and its service entities from chief West Coast container-shipping competitor ports such as Los Angeles-Long Beach; Vancouver, British Columbia; and Seattle. The arrival of intermodal in the 1980s was clearly a game-changing event for the railroad. To pay for it, rate increases were required—never popular, especially with the powerful major carriers, but a step that was nevertheless successfully negotiated in order to assure the railroad's continued viability in this dynamic segment of its business.

The Lakeview line, which runs north from Nisqually Junction to South Tacoma, is part of the former Northern Pacific Prairie Line. The right-hand corner shows a small portion of the Lakewood Industrial Park.

Grain silos operated by the largest customer on the Lakeview line, X-Cel Feeds Inc., in a 2005 photo taken before the track was rebuilt to accommodate Sound Transit commuter trains that now travel south to Lakewood, Washington.

AN ALLIANCE FOR GLOBAL TRADE

Freight rail is a 19th-century industry that continues to be central to 21st-century prosperity. A 2014 study commissioned by the Washington Council on International Trade and BNSF estimated Washington state's freight-rail industry employs more than 342,000 people (more than 10 percent of the state's workforce) and generates an impressive 7.5 percent of the state's entire economic output. Freight rail is responsible for $28.5 billion of the state's economic activity.

The year 2015 ushered in an era of partnership between unlikely allies. The Ports of Seattle and Tacoma, often bitter rivals in competition for customers and cargo, formed the Northwest Seaport Alliance to promote shipping via Puget Sound as the conduit to global ocean trade. The combined Seattle and Tacoma ports will be able to leverage their overall volume as the third-largest gateway in North America, behind Los Angeles–Long Beach and New York–New Jersey.

The strategy enables the Northwest Seaport Alliance to increase the number of international container terminals it provides and maintains, serving the world's largest container vessels in direct competition with ports at Los Angeles–Long Beach; Vancouver, British Columbia; and on the East Coast that are currently leading trans-Pacific trade activity out of North America.

The Seattle and Tacoma ports retain their independence in some lines of operation, but the ability to unify focus on commerce will bring about new efficiency and along with it infrastructure needs—not only at the sea terminals and port roads, but also including jointly coordinated intermodal transport. The pair of ports today promote employment of some 48,000 people, including truckers and rail workers. With the expected increase in freight/cargo volume the ports are expected to see based on the new alliance, employment may well go up, too.

TOWARD THE NEXT CENTURY

Stepchild, cost-of-service business, taxpayer, survivor. Through two world wars and beyond, the Tacoma Municipal Belt Line has evolved from passenger service moving workers to factory and shipbuilding jobs on the Tacoma Tideflats into Tacoma Rail, a self-sustaining freight operation plugged into the global intermodal economy.

Operating under the control of local government has not always made life easy for the railroad and its finances. At times, a lack of strong alliances has kept Tacoma Rail from taking advantage of its geography. In past years, takeover threats affected the railroad's progress and from time to time so did the struggle to establish compensatory switching rates.

The cost of service has often been a bone of contention for the major carriers and the Port of Tacoma. Over time though, Tacoma Rail has developed a much closer relationship with the Port, supporting it globally by enabling the Port to escape costs of most of its rail switching.

Strong economic headwinds have often caused Tacoma Rail to make budget sacrifices or put off upgrades. At times, the loss of a major customer cut into the railroad's earnings. The Great Recession and periods when local markets were weak negatively affected the amount of real traffic in and out of Tacoma.

Expansion of Tacoma Rail's geographical area of service brought with it lingering growing pains and burdensome grant commitments. Passenger operations on the Mountain Division such as the Train to the Mountain, the GrandLuxe, Spirit of Washington Dinner Train, and its own excursions have never been financially rewarding for Tacoma Rail. The decline of industry has affected the outlying lines. The line has never quite fully optimized its use of the Centralia/Chehalis corridor, for example. But for every backward step, such as the death of logging in the 1980s, there seems to have been an evolutionary forward step—intermodal expansion, automobile growth, and recently, crude oil shipped by train and the Northwest Seaport Alliance—to counter the negative effects and give Tacoma Rail and Tacoma's economy a boost.

Since its inception, the rail industry has always been susceptible to a thousand economic and political changes—large and small, global and local—affecting its potential to grow, develop new services, or simply operate profitably. Tacoma Rail is no exception. But it has persevered. Thanks to a visionary management team, it has been flexible, if not downright dogged, in its quest to overcome the many structural and external obstacles that history, politics, and the global economy have put in its way. The railroad has found solutions to keep it running, keep it growing, and keep it prospering.

TR 2200—an Eco Rebuild—
works the Tacoma Rail yard with
Mount Rainier looming beyond,
2014. *Photo by Steve Carter*

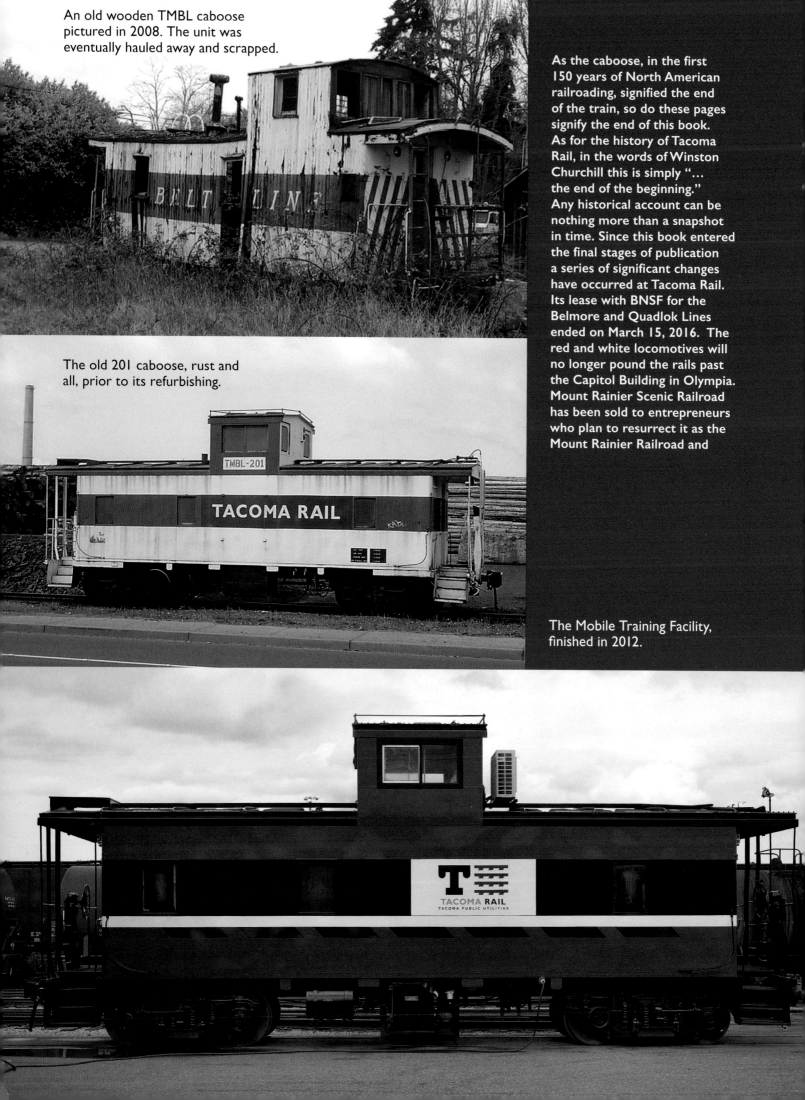

An old wooden TMBL caboose pictured in 2008. The unit was eventually hauled away and scrapped.

The old 201 caboose, rust and all, prior to its refurbishing.

As the caboose, in the first 150 years of North American railroading, signified the end of the train, so do these pages signify the end of this book. As for the history of Tacoma Rail, in the words of Winston Churchill this is simply "…the end of the beginning." Any historical account can be nothing more than a snapshot in time. Since this book entered the final stages of publication a series of significant changes have occurred at Tacoma Rail. Its lease with BNSF for the Belmore and Quadlok Lines ended on March 15, 2016. The red and white locomotives will no longer pound the rails past the Capitol Building in Olympia. Mount Rainier Scenic Railroad has been sold to entrepreneurs who plan to resurrect it as the Mount Rainier Railroad and

The Mobile Training Facility, finished in 2012.

Logging Museum (MRRLM) with visions of re-establishing a vibrant tourist trade in the towns of Elbe and Mineral. The sale of the south end of the C-Line to Chehalis and Lewis County has fallen through, casting an uncertain light on the future of that portion of the Mountain Division. Construction of the Point Defiance Bypass has begun in earnest which will bring Amtrak trains onto the Lakeview Line by 2017, adding a whole new set of challenges to maintaining reliable freight service between South Tacoma and Lakewood. As in the past, Tacoma Rail will rise to meet these challenges and in its second century of operation will exceed anything that could have been imagined in its first one hundred years.

The storage rack for flashing rear-end devices (FRED) is the modern-day equivalent of the caboose track.

The TMBL 1914 was the second-to-last caboose built in North America when Weyerhaeuser ordered three models for the Chehalis Western when it acquired the line from the bankrupt Milwaukee Road in 1980.

Tacoma Rail's 1970s colors featured in the retro look for the Centennial Caboose.

BIBLIOGRAPHY

An Engine of Prosperity: Freight Rail's Pivotal Role in Pacific Northwest's Export Economy.

   Commissioned by the Washington Council on International Trade and BNSF Railway. 2014.

   http://www.vancouverenergyusa.com/assets/engineofprosperity_econreport.pdf

Associated Press. "Tacoma Rail discloses Bakken oil shipment information." June 23, 2014.

Cantlin, David J. *Tacoma Rail (Images of Rail).* Arcadia Publishing. 2013.

Electric Railway Journal. McGraw-Hill Publishing Company. Vol. 49, No. 20. May 19, 1917. P. 940.

Electric Traction Newsletter, Kenfield-Davis Publishing Company. Vol. 16. December 1920. P. 933.

"Forty-three passengers die in a trolley car accident in Tacoma on July 4, 1990." The Free

   Online Encyclopedia of Washington State History,

      www.historylink.org/_content/printer_friendly/pf_output.cfm?file_id=7477

Gaines, William. "Let's examine rail sale idea." *News Tribune* [Tacoma, Wash]. June 21, 2009. A.12.

"General Motors streetcar conspiracy" http://en.wikipedia.org/wiki/General_Motors_streetcar_conspiracy

History business.org

Hunt, Herbert. *Hunt's History of Tacoma.* Chicago, Illinois: S.J. Clarke Publishing Company. 1916.

Jenson, Oliver. *The American Heritage History of Railroads in America.* American Heritage

   Publishing Company. 1975.

Journal of Commerce. "Seattle, Tacoma Seek Intermodal Edge." April 22, 2014.

Morgan, Murray Cromwell and Rosa Morgan. *South on the Sound: An illustrated history of*

   Tacoma and Pierce County. Windsor Publications. 1984.

New York Times. "Plunges One Hundred Feet into a Ravine." July 5, 1900.

Ott, John S. *The Story of the Tacoma Municipal Belt Line Railway.* Tacoma Public Utilities. 1994.

Ott, John S. *The Tacoma Public Utilities Story.* Tacoma Public Utilities. 1993.

The Puget Sound Business Journal. October 8, 2014.

Schwantes, Carlos A. *The Pacific Northwest: An Interpretive History.* University of Nebraska

   Press. 1996.

The Street Railway Journal. Vol. 9, No. 6. June 1893. P. 358, 413.

The Street Railway Review. Chicago: Windsor & Kenfield. Vol. 3. 1893.

Tacoma Daily News. Obituary of Lucian F. Cook. January 17, 1910.

Tacoma Ledger. "City signs for new belt line." October 30, 1924. P. 4.

Tacoma Ledger. "Mayor pulls cord, city's cars start." October 2, 1917. P. 1.

Tacoma News Tribune. "McCune." July 26, 1947.

Tacoma News Tribune. "New Kid on the Dock Turns Heads." January 29, 2005. P. D1.

Tacoma News Tribune. Obituary of Ernest Dolge. November 12, 1959.

Tacoma News Tribune. "Quits Post at Chamber." October 23, 1946.

Tacoma Rail annual reports 1999–2014.

USA Today. "Dinner Train Rolling Again Toward Rainier." August 20, 2017.

Voelpel, Dan. "Sell the railroad, Tacoma, then use proceeds to repair the city's streets."

   News Tribune [Tacoma, Wash]. June 12, 2009. A.12.

Acknowledgment

American Short Line and Regional RR Association

Association of American Railroads

John Gillie, *Tacoma News Tribune*

Chris Gleason, Tacoma Public Utilities

National Railway Historical Society

John Phillips, "Tacoma CityScape," Tacoma TV 12

Port of Tacoma

David Spradling, Austin Public Library

Gary Tarbox, Pacific Northwest Railroad Archive

Washington State Railroads Historical Society

INDEX

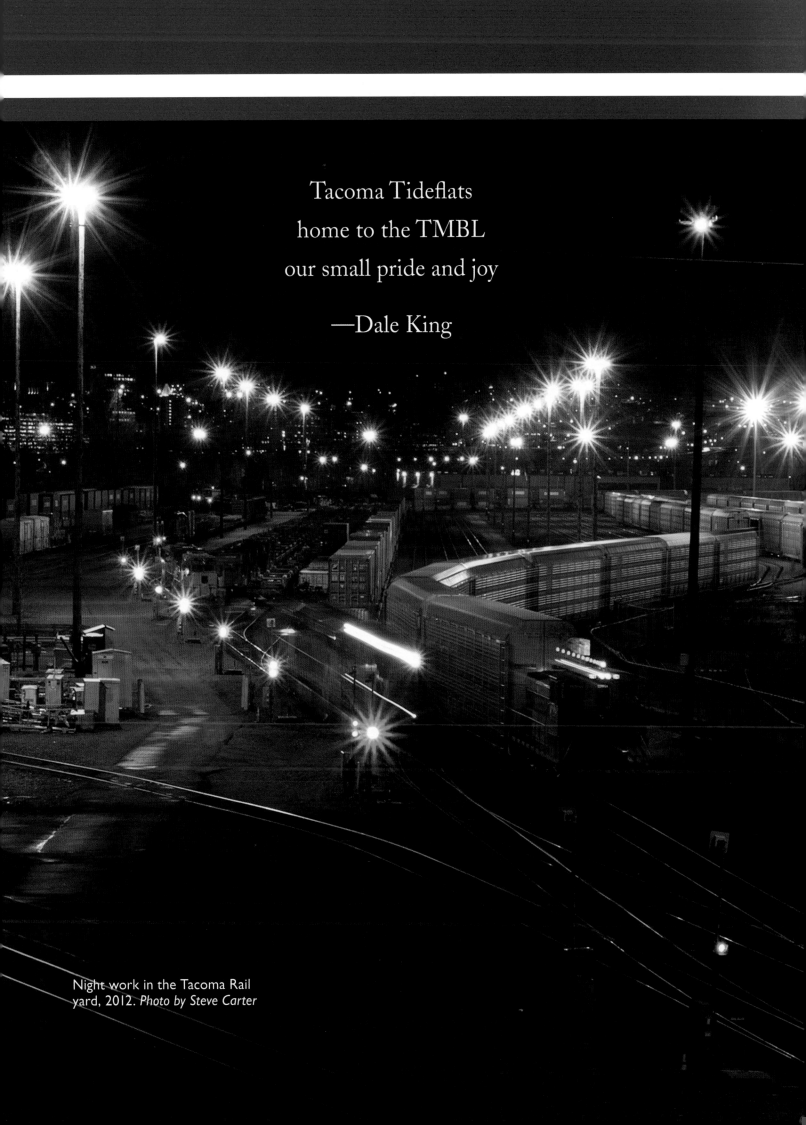

Tacoma Tideflats
home to the TMBL
our small pride and joy

—Dale King

Night work in the Tacoma Rail
yard, 2012. *Photo by Steve Carter*

ABOUT THE AUTHOR

Stuart Wade is a writer and marketing consultant and a former communications executive. He is the author of two books and numerous articles about business, technology, and culture. Stu is equally at ease writing for corporate clients as for stand-up comedians and appreciates the similarities between the two. A devoted husband and father of three boys, the Austin, Texas, resident holds a BA in journalism from Indiana University.

For the next century, Tacoma Rail's newest locomotive 2316 is being rebuilt by Progress Rail, a division of Caterpillar Inc., at their shop in Tacoma's Tideflats. This Tier 3 engine will replace the GP20 2006 as part of a joint venture with the Port of Tacoma made possible by a grant from the U.S. Environmental Protection Agency.